Learning to Love
Differently

a healing pathway for families of addicts

CANDACE HARTZLER, MA/LICDC

ISBN: 978-1-4834-8566-9 (sc)
ISBN: 978-1-4834-8565-2 (e)

Because of the dynamic nature of the Internet, any web addresses or links contained in this book may have changed since publication and may no longer be valid. The views expressed in this work are solely those of the author and do not necessarily reflect the views of the publisher, and the publisher hereby disclaims any responsibility for them.

This book is a work of non-fiction. Unless otherwise noted, the author and the publisher make no explicit guarantees as to the accuracy of the information contained in this book and in some cases, names of people and places have been altered to protect their privacy.

Any people depicted in stock imagery provided by Getty Images are models, and such images are being used for illustrative purposes only. Certain stock imagery © Getty Images.

Lulu Publishing Services rev. date: 06/08/2018

Contents

Acknowledgements vii

About the Author ix

Preface xv

Chapter 1 **Living in the Web of Addiction** 1

An addict in the family, what is it like? Author's personal story. Statistics from National Institute on Drug Abuse. Laura's story. Marketing blitz. How bad is it? Sam Quinones' book. SAMHSA report. How this book can help you to love differently. Intervening vs. enabling. Philip, an addict's story. Your growth depends on five factors. Description of Story Pages. Your first Story Page.

Chapter 2 **Coming to Terms** 23

Planned or unplanned? What is denial? Yours? Theirs? Shelley's story. What is addiction? Disease or mental illness? What do the professionals say? AMA, ASAM, DSM-5, NIDA. The problem of co-occurring disorders. Definition of addiction. Anna, an alcoholics' story. Examining your role. Carolyn's story. Your second Story Page.

Chapter 3 **Codependent Attachment** 43

"Work" of love. Birth of codependency. Codependent symptoms. Kathleen's story. Emotions and codependency. Lois Wilson and Al-Anon. Those hard choices. La-La Land. What codependency is NOT.

Elizabeth's story. Magic word. Jane's story. Third Story Page.

Chapter 4 **Naming the Pain** 63

What is powerlessness? Addiction, if allowed, conquers all. Addiction changes our rules and our roles. An illustrative story. The greatest fear. David, an alcoholic's story. What is surrender? The saturation point. What is acceptance? Attaching language to your feelings. More from Elizabeth's story. The razor blade. Actions. Kyle's story. Your fourth Story Page.

Chapter 5 **What Can You Do?** 83

Step Zero. Brian's story and poem. Rewriting your life circumstances—no blame. Colleen's story. Can you step away? Straight talk with the addicted one. Daniel's story. Enabling or helping? Finding your fear signature. More from Colleen's story. Recovery changes your view. More from Kyle's story. Small steps. Rachael's story. A cheat sheet to reframe responses. Michael's story. Let's not forget the kids. More from Carolyn's story. Your fifth Story Page.

Chapter 6 **Building Spiritual Support** 103

Importance of having a network. Constance's story. Becoming habituated to chains. Giving things up and sharing your truth. Dwayne's story. Who are you your pain? Some questions. Religion or not? Three important constructs. Mental immunity. Doing the work. Five components for establishing a support system. More from Shelley's story. More from Kyle's story. The time has come.

Epilogue 119

Recovery Intentions..123

Short Reminders and Other Things You Need to Know.................125

Resources..131

Acknowledgements

To Steve, whose gifts and talents were stolen by alcoholism. I thank you for all we created together.

To Keith, Bryan and Kristina, who have witnessed, listened, learned and grown into their own beautiful, independent lives. You are the jewels of mine.

To Muriel, a wonderfully bright and loving woman who suffered from the illness of alcoholism. We did a lot of things wrong.

To my husband. For holding my dreams steady with his love and laughter during life and particularly during this writing.

To all those folks through all the years who kept encouraging me "to write that stuff down."

To Rick, my "computer guy." I could not have accomplished this without you. Thank you for your kind teachings.

To all those who shared testimonies in this book. Thank you for paying it all forward.

To my friend and writing partner, Mary Ann. Your encouragement, prayers and wonder at the material covered in this book have supported me beyond measure.

To my soul friend, Molly, and to my spiritual support group. Unending gratitude for all those prayers-in-the-basket.

To Nancy for help in the early days of this manuscript and to Gretchen who helped me bring all the words and all the pages into a new light. Both are editors extraordinaire.

To all those who read and advised. Your support was invaluable.

About the Author

Candace Hartzler holds an undergraduate degree from Otterbein University and a Master's degree in Alcoholism and Drug Abuse Ministry from The Methodist Theological School in Delaware, Ohio. She has completed 400 hours of training in Expressive Arts Therapy from The Person-Centered Expressive Arts Therapy Program in Santa Rosa, California.

Her early years were shaped by familial alcoholism, and she continued to create emotional connections with beautiful people who were alcohol or drug addicted. She has worked a personal recovery program for 35-plus years. She has been a Licensed Chemical Dependency Counselor since 1991 and recently retired from the Family Advocacy counseling position at The Ohio State University, Talbot Hall, Wexner Medical Center Addictions Treatment Unit in Columbus, Ohio. She currently has a private practice at Gentle Steps Counseling in Clintonville, Ohio.

She has worked with all populations in her counseling career, including teens, women's gender-specific treatment groups, aftercare for families, family education, intensive outpatient treatment groups for both women and men, and mixed gender inpatient treatment groups.

Candace was a chosen presenter in 2012 at the National Conference on Addiction Disorders held in Washington, D.C.; the focus for her workshop was Family Addiction. She has written numerous articles for Ohio Bar Lawyer's Quarterly magazine and published an article in an Online Channel, PsychCentral, entitled "Let's Not Forget the Kids," August 2017.

She has served as faculty member at the Addictions Studies Institute, The Ohio State University, and her essay "Creativity and Healing," was selected from a compilation of articles from Personal Transformation Magazine for publication in Soulful Living: The Process of Personal Transformation, published by Health Communications, Inc., (1999). Others included in the book are Deepak Chopra, Bernie Siegel, M.D., Jean Huston, Ph.D. and John O'Donohue.

ENDORSEMENTS for *Learning to Love Differently, a healing pathway for families of addicts*

Candace Hartzler has written a powerful, personal and highly useful book. *Learning to Love Differently* addresses the painful challenge of addicts and their families. Drawing on her own experiences of growing up in an alcoholic home, as well as on her professional practice, she illuminates a pathway to healing that encompasses practical and effective approaches.

The author uses clinical vignettes throughout the book to illustrate both failures and successes as loved ones learn to separate the addict's pain from their own. This book comes highly recommended.

Tom Pepper, MD, Addiction Psychiatrist

* * * *

Our national epidemic of heroin addiction allows us to forget that other drug addictions are still alive and well. The total number of those negatively affected (families, friends, co-workers) increases each year. In times like these, we are so ready for a book that can detail the circular connection between the addict and codependent. *Learning to Love Differently, a healing pathway for families of addicts*, guides families with detailed information, offers examples from family members and gives helpful exercises at the end of each chapter. Candace Hartzler has given us a one-stop-shop that will provide readers with a complete and thorough map to recovery and health. It is a resource that I look forward to providing my clients, as it "connects the dots" of the family healing process.

Victoria J. Johnson, LICDC, LPCC

* * * *

Learning to Love Differently, a pathway of healing for families of addicts, brought both tears and laughter. It is a beautiful and brave look at the soul disease of addiction, sheds light on the controversial topic of addiction currently gripping our country. This book holds no blame/shame for the addict or the codependent. Love is always the best answer, but addiction complicates life for all involved in the addict's web of pain. This book offers a healthier definition and charts a path for family and friends to begin their own healing journey.

Lisa Lavelle, M.Ed., LSW, LICDC-CS

* * * *

Learning to Love Differently, a pathway of healing for families of addicts, illuminates a path toward personal recovery for families that live in a constant state of hurt, fear, and confusion . The book gives permission not to know what is best for our addicted loved ones and teaches how to stop making decisions for them. It describes powerlessness as a form of freedom and detachment as a form of love. Hartzler's words guide us towards making decisions based on what is best for ourselves and outlines how to establish a healthier relationship with a loved one suffering from a substance use disorder. The book leads us through a deep discovery of how to be compassionate with ourselves.

Jill D., recovering family member with two sons in long-term recovery

* * * *

Candace Hartzler knows about relationships. *Learning to Love Differently, a pathway of healing for families of addicts* with study guide included, will help anyone to increase their potential for a successful trip through the difficult journey of loving an addict. Highly recommended for anyone in treatment for addiction or codependence.

Sharon Endicott, MA/M.Div.

* * * *

I have worked in the field of addictions and mental health for 30 years. *Learning to Love Differently, a pathway of healing for families of addicts,* communicates simply and directly what I try to teach my clients. So much of the literature has been directed to one population (spouses, children, etc.) to the exclusion of others while Hartzler incorporates examples from across the spectrum. The exercises at the end of each chapter help readers explore their personal truths and guide them in making valuable lifestyle changes. I will utilize this book in my practice.

Barbara Brigham, LISW, LICDC

* * * *

In *Learning to Love Differently, a pathway of healing for families of addicts,* Hartzler demonstrates a keen understanding of the unrelenting pain of living with the devastating effects of alcoholism and drug addiction. She invites readers to reflect on what they are learning while enveloping them in a warm blanket of compassion and empathy. I'm sure Captain Jack's garden is flourishing somewhere.

Ray Iron, PH.D., PCC-S, LICDC-CS

Preface

My life was shaped by family addiction, but it took decades for me to see and accept that fact. Mother's emotional life had already been patterned by my father's drinking episodes before I was born. Although there would be bright spots along the path of family life, our denial and confusion grew as his drinking slid headlong into addiction to alcohol.

During my early and middle adulthood, I continued to create emotional connections to beautiful people who were addicted to alcohol or other drugs. The painful lessons continued until one day I stopped scratching my head, ceased blaming others, and began the journey of growth and change.

This book is a primer and a workbook of sorts. It also acts as a mirror, helping you see and recognize your place in the addict's life. Exercises and visual images at the end of each chapter offer a way to personalize the information in the chapters. These pages are the ones I wish I'd had access to all those years ago while I sat smack-dab in the middle of codependency, not knowing how to talk about or heal the mental suffering. This book exposes family dysfunction connected to an addicted loved one and shows how pain permeates a relational system. It invites you to tend what you can, which is yourself. It does not overwhelm you with information. Instead, it offers a starting place. It serves as a building block, provides a base for you to begin taking charge of your life and allows you to turn the page on how you love the addicted loved one. It uses the terms alcoholic, addict and substance use disorder interchangeably.

It is important to remember that loved ones addicted to alcohol or other drugs can and do heal. A son addicted to heroin needs hope and healthy focus more than clean needles. A daughter addicted to alcohol needs to hear the truth of how her out-of-control drinking is affecting you. She does not need your sympathy or your enabling.

Current media focus on addiction provides information about the scope of our nation's problems for the ones addicted but communicates little about a family's need to heal its relational system. Like addicts, families can and do heal. But addicts and families can't heal one another. Each must feel the pain of that humbling place called powerlessness and forge separate healing pathways.

Applause for you from this end of recovery as you begin building a new, loving, and accepting framework for family healing. You are the brave ones. You are the informed ones.

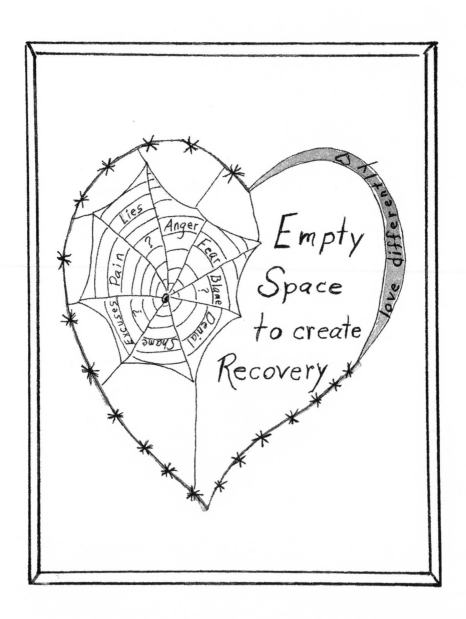

Living in the Web of Addiction

How can we ever do that which
seems impossible? Taking a class, quitting
a job, leaving a destructive relationship
behind, asking for help; none
of these can we do alone or with ease.
❖ *Each Day a New Beginning,* Hazelden Meditation Series

So there I sat all smart and smug in the front row. It was my first day of class in the Alcoholism and Drug Abuse Ministry Master's Degree program at The Methodist Theological School in Delaware, Ohio. I felt like twins living in a single body. One part of me wanted to run while another part silently screamed, "Stick around, you need this." I had loved more than my share of alcoholics and addicts, and at last I would be able to figure them out. I stuck around, and although I had

1

attended a few A.A. meetings with my father and even a sprinkling of Al-Anon meetings, I had no idea of the depth or breadth of personal recovery miles I had yet to travel.

I sat through that first day of class not knowing what I didn't yet know. I may have lacked education about the construct of family addiction, but I sure didn't lack feelings. My heart was filled to capacity with fear, blame, and shame created by years of living inside family addiction. Those over-the-top folks who seemed to rank drinking or drug use over relational needs had turned my life into an emotional crazy quilt. It was easy to point my finger at all the drunk and drug addicted people, convinced they were responsible for all that felt wrong in my life. But part of what I didn't know on that squirmy day, was that I was drunk too. Not on substances, but on those rocky emotions that fill the hearts of family members who live with addiction. I was a nerve-wracked newbie, a fresh face sitting in the front row of a new way of being.

How it all started

I was born into a substance abusing household, raised in the house that Jack built. Jack was my father, and our household was chock-full of the unspoken rules of his alcoholism: don't talk or trust or feel, remain silent lest the walls tumble down around you. It was the late 1960s in small-town Ohio. The term "alcoholic" had not yet come of age, so all of us—Mother, Dad, my five brothers, and I—didn't know what we didn't know. We had no language for Dad's drinking. We had no words to describe the soft parts of ourselves plowed under by his alcoholism. We saw only the painful misuse of booze: no sane or safe toasts at family gatherings, no classy clinking of crystal goblets on holidays. We knew nothing about healing and had no models for seeking help outside our household. Dad's drinking episodes ruled our moods. We were a stiff bunch of people trying to stay alive in a family system framed by illness.

My mother blamed Dad for his drinking, and he blamed her for giving him reason to drink. They spent so much time in the whirl of blame that it would, in the end, suffocate their vows and create mountains of confusion for the six of us sitting in the kid seats.

Dad drank, and we sat huddled on the edges of his drinking escapades. We watched Mother become bent on stopping Dad's drinking while he remained bent on claiming his "right to drink whenever and whatever the hell I want." Although tension in our house was palpable, we had no idea what to call it. We were just kids, and so we spread smiles across our tiny Mayberry-like town.

We were a cute, handsome, and fun-loving brood of children. If our neighbors knew of our dad's drinking issues, they never let on. My brothers and I acted out the no-talk rule, but each of us experienced Dad's drinking differently. Each would create a different story in response to what the family could not discuss. Our mother shielded us as best she could, but years of fear and neglect finally took their toll.

Our petite, witty, dark-haired mother finally broke from the pressure of holding tight to her codependent role. It happened in the spring on a warm Saturday afternoon. After twenty-five years of following all the rules, after all the cover-ups and fear of watching her husband drink his way in and out of paychecks as a grave-digger, farmer, maintenance man, painting contractor, bulldozer operator, vitamin salesman, and construction worker, she broke down and broke open. Mother loaded her husband's urine-soaked bed sheets into a black garbage bag, tossed the bag into the trunk of her car and drove to Bianchi's Bar, where dad sat precariously on top of his favorite bar stool.

"Here you go, Jack," she said, as she slid the bag along the wooden floor. "Your mess, not mine." And she slammed the door behind her.

Sliding the years of frustration across the barroom floor was an enormous first step for mother and public shaming for our father. Dad had a bad-and-getting-worse-by-the-day-illness, but we didn't treat him like a man with an illness. We were hurt and confused by his choice to drink the way he did, and again, we didn't know what we didn't know. Public shaming does not heal any illness, least of all a person with a substance use disorder. But our behaviors back then were born from ignorance, hurt, and frustration. Even though Mother's caretaking days were coming to an end, there would be one last calamity.

A month later, our mother pulled my little brother's Louisville Slugger from beneath the couch and hit my drunken, oh-so-ill-and-raging-father quite solidly over the head. She filed for divorce soon after, found Al-Anon, church, her God, and a great amount of acceptance and healing. Dad would eventually find A.A. and remain sober for twenty-seven years. My brothers and I would also find our way into creating lives based on new rules for the road.

My father's brain and body were being systematically poisoned by the excessive use of alcohol. But he was more than a man with an undiagnosed illness. He was also an intelligent, charismatic, handsome, hard-working man with dreams of his own, and while his family watched his dreams smash solidly against those bottles of bourbon, all we knew how to do was nurse our own suffering.

Dad's addiction had snagged us all. His family lacked people who knew how not to blame him. We lacked information. We lacked insight. We lacked faith. We lacked support. We lacked ourselves. And we surely lacked him. We didn't know he had a chronic illness. The man who dreamed of becoming a writer or an airline pilot or anything but who he had become could not stay away from the bottle, and he was like so many others. The National Institute on Drug Abuse reports that illicit and prescription drugs and alcohol contribute to the death of more than 90,000 Americans each year. That's nine times the entire population of Sedona, Arizona, wiped out every single year.

Statistics regarding addiction to illicit and prescription drugs and alcohol are easier to calculate than its impact on family members. I was one of those family members, still gripping my own lopsided stories connected to my father's and husband's bottles of bourbon, when I sat squirming in the front row of class. Sharing my story had never been in the picture. I was an introvert. Thinking about asking for help outside my tight little life sent shivers up my spine. I was sure of only one thing: if my father, husband, and a few other close relatives would just stop drinking and using drugs, my world would spin as it should. I was wrong. My life was up to me, not to my loved one's addictions.

Laura's story

"*Nights were the worst: his screaming; angry words and hitting; her crying; and the crashing sounds of destruction. Did he think I wouldn't hear all that because it was late at night and I had gone to my room hours earlier? Did he care?*

"*Sometimes it would continue as they came upstairs. His threats became even more real as his words became more distinct. I trembled under the covers and clutched my pillow for security. I was their only child and the solitary witness to those nights of terror.*

"*My mom and I never talked to anyone about what was going on in our home. We kept my father's drinking episodes secret and showed the world only our smiles. I've reconnected with my best friends from that time and shared my story with them. They didn't have a clue about my home life.*

"*It was our norm, a few days of peace when he was occasionally away, and back to hell when he returned. My mom endured, wouldn't leave him because no one in her Catholic family had ever gotten a divorce. I don't ever remember her trying to explain things or help me feel protected. He was a violent alcoholic, and she was afraid to leave him. He said he would find us and kill us if we left.*

"*My bedwetting didn't stop until I reached my teens. My hatred and fear of him didn't stop until recently, and I'm in my 60s.*"

The marketing blitz

Alcohol is a liquid drug, although not marketed as such. The alcohol industry spends billions of dollars each year marketing alcohol as a substance connected with health, pleasure, and aliveness. The public becomes a bullseye for marketing strategists who, of course, will not market the truth, the whole truth, or even a small bit of the truth. Profit is their bottom line. They want to sell a product, so they don't focus on the harmful impact of alcohol or other addictive substances. You won't see an ad featuring a man too intoxicated to perform sexually. You won't see a young woman passed out and vulnerable on the sofa in a fraternity house. And you won't see a toddler cowering in the corner while her intoxicated parents drink straight from a bottle of Jim Beam while they scream at one another over their lack of finances.

Marketers may include an occasional warning about misuse, almost always in small print, or an admonishment to use alcohol or other drugs responsibly. Ads feature pretty people drinking Grey Goose or Corona or Johnnie Walker Scotch in glamorous settings. Backdrops are often dreamy landscapes or luxurious parties showing glasses full of enticing liquids.

Of course, direct-to-consumer pharmaceutical ads in magazines and on television always show positive images of attractive people using medications or mood-altering drugs—some very powerful—to roll through their days or nights. Even though some drugs are more dangerous than others, the paradigm is the same for all addictive drugs. Once the susceptible is hooked, compulsion builds, and when the user becomes addicted, he will sneak, lie, dodge, and steal things, money and time to maintain a relationship with his preferred drug or drugs. Those favorite drugs will kill off his ability to live life productively. Addictive behaviors do not produce happy, spirit-filled lives. The addict's use of drugs, illicit or prescribed, also weakens his family's well-being. Until family members find their way out of addiction, they follow the patterns dictated by addiction and continue to crawl around the web spun by a loved one's destructive use of substances.

The scope of addiction: how bad is it?

The widespread growth of opiate addiction affecting our nation is getting much press and raising the culture's awareness of addiction's deadly dynamics. The book *Dreamland: The True Tale* of *America's Opiate Epidemic*, written by Sam Quinones offers a full view of how and why America's consumption of narcotics is higher than any other nation in the world. The information provided by Quinones is startling: "Between 2002 and 2011, 25 million Americans used prescription pills non-medically. Amid all this, opiate users began to get younger." Another way to look at those numbers: The Ohio State University's football stadium is the 3rd largest stadium in the United States, seating just shy of 105,000 people. The number of Americans abusing prescription pills in that nine-year period would fill the stadium 238 times.

Quinones writes about how the economic issues of our nation's middle class, coupled with the sloppy/reckless marketing of pharmaceutical opiates, created a seedbed for disaster. The current drug epidemic was born from that coupling. His book is an excellent read and highly recommended for those who want to trace the history of our nation's widespread drug problems.

Perhaps you have read about the legal issues faced by Purdue Pharma. In 2007, the drug company pleaded guilty to federal charges of misrepresenting the abuse/addiction potential of the drug OxyContin. Part of the plea deal included their commitment to reformulate the drug. The reformulation made OxyContin difficult to crush, snort, smoke or inject. Drug issue solved?

Not really. A large-scale study published in 2017 by the National Bureau of Economic Research found that although the non-medical use of OxyContin decreased by forty percent after the 2010 formulation, heroin overdose deaths increased threefold in subsequent years. As sad as all our current opiate/heroin addiction problems are, perhaps if any good is coming out of the epidemic is that addiction is finally getting the attention it so deserves.

Heroin has become a particularly popular drug. It's much cheaper than opiates and is highly addictive. It creates a chemical stronghold on users sooner rather than later and unfortunately is readily available in small towns and large cities. Fentanyl is a powerful synthetic opioid, similar to morphine but is 50 to 100 times more potent. Non-pharmaceutical Fentanyl has wound its way through the illicit drug trade and when mixed with heroin, increases the risk for overdose.

Those drugs, when abused, can lead to much pain and suffering. But let us not overlook the impact alcohol has on our nation's families. Alcohol use is more socially acceptable but is in no way an innocent bystander. A 2017 report prepared by the Center for Behavioral Health Statistics and Substance Abuse and Mental Health Services Administration (SAMHSA) quoted on Addiction Now, (an online site) that 20.2 million adults had a past year substance use disorder in 2014. Of that 20.2 million, 6.2 million had an illicit drug addiction compared with 16.3 million with an addiction to alcohol. In spite of the high degree of suffering created by opiate use/abuse/addiction, alcohol still wins the award of the most-abused drug.

The pain of it all

We can no longer hide the problems beneath our 3,000 square feet homes, our Smart TVs, our laptops, or our iPhones. No more secrets and no more denial. Addiction is killing our children and harming the hearts of families. The problems are on every street corner in America and all levels of society. Our nation is hurting and families need answers. The challenges of alcohol and other drug addiction are far reaching but not impossible to comprehend. Families who make it into recovery rooms will discover that hiding hurts them more than truth-telling. Parents and loved ones who open their minds and hearts can learn how to separate truth from the lies told by the addict. Creating a support system for yourself allows you to gain a foothold and to form a base for healthier decision making.

This book was born out of a lecture series I created to help educate family members. I had been an addictions counselor for many years before the opiate epidemic hit, working with all populations, providing care to adolescents, adults, gender-specific programs and family programs. Through the years, I watched family programs fall by the wayside. Inpatient settings, as well as outpatient settings, offered little more than brief education sessions, hardly enough to scratch the surface of a family's true needs. There were a variety of reasons, I suppose, but mainly programs were cut to shave costs. The face-to-face work so prevalent during the 1980s slowly left the treatment scene.

When I began offering family support during my tenure as Family Advocacy Counselor in Columbus, Ohio, The Ohio State University, Talbot Hall, I was amazed at the number of family members who showed up night after night. Some attendees had loved ones in treatment, and

8

they were hungry for ways to help their family members; others came from the public sector merely to gather information about addiction. Nursing students and other college students studying for counseling degrees attended to gain front-line knowledge about alcoholism and drug addiction. Even some recovering addicts attended and their input was invaluable.

The pain in the room could be felt. Fathers had questions. Mothers had tears. The children who attended squirmed in their seats. A few of them offered input. A mother would ask, "But what did I do wrong?" A father would rail, "I didn't raise my kid to shoot dope." A sister would confess, I've done some drugs with him, but I stopped. Why didn't he? Is this my fault?"

Week after week for five years, I witnessed the pain and confusion. I also began to see change happen. The more education and support family members received, the more openly they shared with me and with one another. The group meeting became a place for each to develop a voice. Pain that was so tangible in the beginning gave way to an understanding of their personal dynamic. New understanding permitted members to create boundaries with their loved one. Members worked at their own pace. Some were ripe and ready to begin their work when they stepped into the lecture hall. Others had stronger codependent ties that took longer to loosen. But given permission, invitation, and education about the far-reaching tentacles of a loved one's addiction, families began their healing process.

Never underestimate the power of open hearts and minds. That combination fuels change. Week after week, I witnessed audience members become more willing to share their tears and their fears. They became more willing to risk standing up to their addicted loved one, particularly when we couched family recovery stories in loving terms: **"You don't have to stop loving, but it's important to learn how to love the addicted one differently."** That statement was repeated each week, and I felt privileged to watch expressions—and behaviors—change as family members became more soft and open.

So how about you?

Weaving your emotional world into the addict's chaotic one is as natural as breathing. She uses drugs, and you hurt. His drinking is out of control, and you tremble with fear. I know this because before I taught it I lived it from the inside out. All those loved ones who were addicted in my family system, particularly my husband and my father just needed to stop using so I could feel sane. I told them that. Over and over. And over and over, I stood frozen in place while each one broke promises to quit using.

No matter an addict's drug of choice—alcohol, opiates, cocaine, heroin, marijuana, Fentanyl, or other mood altering substances— addiction deserves respect. Not admiration, mind you, but respect. It breaks lives into tiny pieces and feeds on denial, confusion, fear, shame, and blame. Addiction creates a web of worry and concern that will snag you time and again. Addiction compromises all the principles governing love and trust. Your emotions, as well as your behavior, become difficult to manage.

You may find yourself blaming the addict for becoming addicted: "If she had just never taken that first drink." "He should have known better." "He chose to use, so this is what he deserves."

You point fingers, shame, argue, spew wrath and anger at the irrational behaviors of your out-of-control family member. The more you hurt, the more out of control you feel and the more you try to control the one who is addicted. The closer you stand to the one addicted, the more misshapen your inner life becomes. And it is that inner life that creates your behaviors. It's like a row of dominoes; everyone falls.

You play the game by the addict's rules until you create new and healthier boundaries. Yes, addiction is serious business. It can also become a gateway for your spiritual and emotional growth. It can also lay the groundwork for deep and personal healing.

Loving an addict is painful. Addiction makes it difficult for the heart to trust and the mind to see. Lies and denial form the framework of addiction. But you can learn to love differently. You can find out how to:

- Examine the illness
- Express love, care, and concern without giving your power away to the one addicted
- Offer support without creating a soft place for the addict to fall
- Separate from your unhealthy attachment to your addicted loved one
- Accept and cope with the illness
- Stop taking the illness of addiction personally
- Be gentle with yourself
- Trust in yourself and your God, and even in other people
- Become a healthy family member
- Open up your heart and mind to new ways of being in this complex world
- Identify your needs and find ways to meet them without harm to yourself or others
- Identify and accept what is not yours to fix
- Nurture and love yourself
- Break the cycle of codependency
- Be true to who you are
- Become grateful for the lessons inherent in loving and detaching from your addict

In short, you can become a better, more open, more loving and stronger version of yourself. Yes. You can.

What you'll need to do

People not yet in recovery create all sorts of relational and spiritual atrocities for the sake of their preferred substances. Men and women with a substance abuse disorder are very often excellent people—sensitive, intelligent, and caring—but so caught in the illness of addiction and by their need to remain high or intoxicated that they can't see or feel the destruction all around them.

I remember the night I came home from a date and my father was in the kitchen leaning against the Formica countertop. His time at the bar after work had left him in pretty poor shape. I was headed for the stairs, and I wanted to get up to my bedroom as fast as I could. His speech was slurred, his eyes glassy. "Your mother doesn't understand. She gets so damn mad at me, but she doesn't understand that I need to drink. I don't know how to stop."

His words fell like rocks around my feet. I was sixteen and had no idea how to respond. A dad is supposed to need his family, not his alcohol. I just wanted to escape what I was seeing and feeling. I didn't have the information I needed, and I sure didn't have a way to give language to anything that was happening in my inner or outer worlds. I high tailed it upstairs and never breathed a word of that conversation to another soul.

It would take many years for my family to gain insight into Dad's illness, to begin to hold him accountable for his drinking, and to claim the right to heal ourselves.

This is what's real: if you don't move out of the way of pain, your crazy feeling states will trump your ability to trust in this beautiful place called life. If you decide not to change, if you keep the threads of your life tied to the addict's, holding his hand while you both vie for control, both of you may perish. You will remain reactive and lost while your loved one does what active users do best: live down the rabbit hole, separated from life's beauty and meaning. You don't have to live down there with him.

The process of coming to terms with your circumstances may feel arduous and daunting, even as the carnage of addiction mounts in your life, so it's important to remember that no matter what you do, there is no pain-free ticket to take you into your healing process. There are pain and discomfort either way you travel. It's so much easier to keep your eyes on the one actively addicted than to take a look at your own life. Or so it seems. But killing off parts of your life while bearing the cross of another's addiction will, in time, begin to hurt just a bit too much.

You have choices: intervene or enable?

Addiction in a family system creates chaos. It also invites choice. Addiction throws your love out of balance, and maintaining family stability becomes an art form that needs to be cultivated and refined. Maintaining family health is hard work under the best of circumstances. Slide your son's addiction to heroin into the mix, or your husband's use of alcohol, and you will be confronted with the task of choice. Do you want to be the intervening family member, one who can influence change? Or do you want to remain the passive enabler?

An intervening family member will step up, gather information about addiction and codependency, and seek advice and support from professionals. When you choose the role of an intervening family member, you explore online resources focused on addiction and seek support from others who have the skills needed to navigate family addiction. You confront the user's behaviors and become more adept at changing your own. This book will help you to begin making those changes. It will increase your awareness of the games played by addicts. It will also outline strategies for you to rewrite your role in your loved one's life.

An enabling family member sits tight, does what the addict wants, believes what the user says, and goes out of his or her way to offer aid. We all fall victim to enabling for a time, so you need feel no shame about ways you have aided or abetted. You didn't know what you didn't know. But standing in place with an addict after negative consequences continue to climb is a sure-fire way to lose sight of your soul and strip meaning from your life.

Each user carries his unique story, but all who become addicted share a lot in common. Although you do not need to know all the sordid details of your loved one's story, rest assured his or her story is similar to others who are addicted. Depending on the drug of choice, addiction is a fast-track to pain. The adage about leading a horse to water fits your role with the user. Your son, daughter, spouse, nephew, niece, or grandchild will find ways to use, despite all your attempts to make them stop.

Philip's story

"My name is Philip, and I am in long-term recovery. I have not used any mind or mood altering chemicals since August 16, 2009.

"I began using alcohol and other drugs at the age of 14, initially smoking marijuana and drinking alcohol. My drugs of choice became heroin, Dextromethorphan (DXM) and marijuana. I didn't enjoy taking only one kind of substance as much as mixing a bunch of different drugs at the same time. My disease progressed rapidly from the onset, leaving me in full-blown addiction within six months of my first use. The first time I got high, something clicked inside my brain, convincing me of all the things I had been missing, and I knew I wanted to be high every moment for the rest of my life.

"My parents confronted me within 30 days of my first use. They disposed of my drugs and mandated completion of a treatment program. My parents proved to be the single greatest barrier to my active addiction. They drug tested and breathalyzed me regularly and sent me to four different treatment programs and a boarding school. They monitored me as closely as possible, restricting my access to money and harmful peer associates. Nothing, however, could have stopped me from getting high. I loved getting high more than I loved my family or friends.

"I was absolutely ruthless to anyone who tried to stand in the way of my use. My parents took the brunt of pain: the horror of finding your son overdosing or attempting suicide is unexplainable. As the brother of an addict, I have experienced the overwhelming grief and insanity of watching a loved one lose every trait I admired about him. I hurt my loved ones in this same way.

"By the end of using, I was homeless and penniless. I had lost all my friends, and my family would barely interact with me. I was led to recovery by the fellowship of Narcotics Anonymous. I began attending N.A. meetings while I was still using. I would get high before, during, and after meetings. But at least I showed up. That was a massive factor for me. When I was finally ready to embrace this new way of life, I was already where I needed to be. People in the rooms hugged me, told me to keep coming back, and I did.

"I believe addiction is a disease of the mind and body, characterized by physical *symptoms of dependence and tolerance, as well as the cognitive-behavioral symptoms of obsession and compulsion. I got sober not necessarily because I hit bottom, but because I had an awakening. I remember one day having the thought, "Every time I use drugs, I end up in the same place: destitute and suicidal. Maybe if I don't get high, I won't end up in those places." People had said that to me over and over again all through my years of using, but the idea still seemed completely novel to me. I finally had just enough surrender and open-mindedness to accept the program of Narcotics Anonymous.*

"My greatest recovery challenge is learning to survive my feelings/impulses without acting on them. Sometimes when I feel lonely or inadequate or embarrassed, I want to act out on codependency, anger, or ego. Recovery helps me learn how to deal with those feelings without causing harm to myself or others. I attend N.A. meetings regularly, have a home group, am active in service, have a sponsor, and sponsor others."

Philip entered recovery when Philip was ready. While his parents had planted seeds for his recovery by detaching with love as he became "homeless and penniless," Philip dealt with his substance use disorder in his own time. His loved ones found strength and focus when they reached out to others for healing. Watching from the sidelines as a loved one loses the ability to create shelter or a make a living should not be done alone or in secret. Family members need to spend time garnering their own healthy support.

If you don't stake claim to your healing, you risk becoming as sick as the one suffering from addiction. When you realize that, you'll be ready to start doing the work of creating new boundaries around the love you feel for the one addicted. On the rough days, when you stand confused—again—or angry—again, remember that unweaving your life from the addict's is not a simple or pretty journey. It will bring along new rules for your life, give you a GPS of sorts to guide you along the path of compassion and self-understanding. A bumpy ride, yes, but one that holds more promise than remaining a passenger in the addict's drunken one.

If you stay on your healing path, you will see more clearly how complicated it is to live with an addict. Yes, you will watch the addict suffer, and yes, you will continue to fail at getting him sober. You cannot make another person heal. You cannot talk someone out of addiction. You cannot know what the addict's compulsivity feels like inside his brain. You cannot expect your pain or your sense of powerlessness to be the key to anything but your own healing process. The addict's willingness to stop using and begin healing will come when it comes. Stop standing around waiting for it. Work on yourself.

How to use this book

It's time for you to get your due: the information you need to start healing your end of the pain. You need new rules and new guidelines. It's time to take eyes off the addicted loved one and place focus wholeheartedly on ways to change your codependent dynamics. This book will define codependency, help you rewrite your role, and guide your healing journey. You will hear from me and from others who have stood where you are standing, who have lived inside an addict's story. Stories from others help normalize feelings. Reading others' stories is how you begin seeing your own. Others' stories will ease your suffering and shed light on your path.

You have just read a part of Philip's story, and you will hear from other recovering men and women. Many can and do, get sober. Their stories will broaden your understanding of the addict's side, and bring hope to the possibilities for your loved one's story.

Learning to Love Differently shows you, the codependent, how to obtain emotional sobriety. The courageous work of pulling yourself away from the one abusing substances, claiming your right to alter your course and mend the hurts, belongs to you and only you. Whether your addict stops using, seeks change, or continues along the soul-blocking path of active addiction, your work is your work. Plain and simple. But not easy.

The tasks will take time, and you'll need ways to anchor the healing principles of family recovery. This book outlines those principles while providing strength and support for your journey. It will help you name and explore your emotions as you tunnel your way through the barriers created by addiction.

All people affected by family addiction benefit from looking inside their beautiful but bereft selves. Bringing to light ways you've compromised your values and unearthing the lies you've lived (and told to others) will provide impetus to continue your healing. Gazing into your emotional world will help you see how addiction bleeds onto whoever is standing close.

The web that binds you to the addict remains intact until you are ready to move out of those seductive relational dynamics. These pages will help you loosen those ties that bind.

So much stays hidden for so long. As you begin to uncover the peculiarities of love and family addiction, your growth will depend on five factors:

1. How willing you are to heal your unhealthy attachment to another's addiction
2. How much insight you gain about your placement in your loved one's addiction
3. How many harmful threads you are willing to clip
4. How many capital-T truths you are ready to see and feel
5. How much consultation you seek from people outside your family system

You can't control the addict's life, but you can surely learn to direct your own. You can find solid footing and places to stand, pause, and deep breathe. You can explore the rocky terrain of family addiction and recovery. You can detach from the addict's story if you are willing to take a good, hard look at your own. That's how your healing will happen.

What is your story?

This book will help you explore your connection to a loved one's addiction through the creation of Story Pages. At the close of each chapter, invitation and guidance are offered, asking you to write and reflect on what you see, know and feel. Story Pages are where you begin exploring and expressing your truth. They are journaling's first cousin. Kathleen Adams, LPC, RPT, Founder and Director of The Center for Journal Therapy, is an excellent resource regarding the power of journal writing for those who desire self-directed change. She writes in *Journal to the Self:* "In moments of ecstasy, in moments of despair, the journal remains an impassive silent friend. Its potential as a tool for holistic mental health is unsurpassed."

Inside you is a gold mine, a rich resource for language, for words. Pulling out those feelings, thoughts, and experiences, languaging them onto your Story Pages will bring insight and heightened self-awareness. The words you put on paper will facilitate change and recovery. Story Pages are where you discover your old story and begin writing a new one.

Expressive writing is an easy, no-fail process. You can't do it wrong. The words grow out of your life experiences. Perfectionism, concern for punctuation, spelling or "getting it right," need not hinder your process. "Perfectionism is the voice of the oppressor," claims author Anne Lamott. And you have been oppressed long enough. Let the word fly. Expressive writing is for your eyes only. Please find a way to keep all you write in a private folder, journal or another restricted resource so you can be comfortable with expressing your truths. No one is going to grade it, judge it, blame it, or shape it into something else. It is yours. Remember, you aren't here to change the addict's story. You are here to explore and change your own.

Story Pages

We hide so much of what we feel through the careful use of talk. We become adept at scripting our responses to please the outside world that our real spirits become confused by our façade, what we want people to see, to know, and to hear. Creating Story Pages taps into the richness of your inside story and is a private and non-linear process. Expressive writing deepens your connection to self, adding both depth and dimension to your relationship with your loved one's addiction and with your codependency. Story Pages help you get to know and befriend yourself.

In Lewis Carrol's *Alice's Adventures in Wonderland*, the following dialogue takes place:

"Would you tell me please, which way I ought to go from here?"

"That depends a good deal on where you want to go," said the cat.

"I don't much care where...," said Alice.

"Then it doesn't matter which way to go," said the cat.

---Lewis Carroll, *Alice in Wonderland*

Very rarely is there a linear path toward healing. So if you "don't much care," if you don't declare intention for wellness and health, you lose your footing quickly, and healing is full of slippery places. The Story Page exercises show ways to begin writing out the old story so you can pencil in a new one. Addiction is the great annihilator of all things sane. Your wellness calls for action, not complacency. Guaranteed: your addict will not wake up one morning, tap you on the shoulder and hand over your healing in a beautifully wrapped package. You need to create it, write it, learn it, live it, move through it and forgive it. And yes. You can do all of that.

* * * * *

Your first Story Page: Is as simple as answering the questions below. Write with any method or form that pleases you. Grab a blank journal, a blank legal pad, iPad or another tablet, or your computer and just begin answering the questions:

- What spoke to you in this chapter?
- Where did you feel the "aha!" moments?
- Can you describe where you are now by creating a title? If your current life was a book, what would the title be?
- What are your current feelings about your addicted loved one?

Fictional Alice didn't much care where she was going. Do you care where you are going?

Where do you want to go from here? Consider those questions, scratch down answers. Then move on to the next Big Three:

1. **Where have I been?** Write three or four words that describe your experiences with addiction/alcoholism. Then flesh out details. What do you see when you look back? What does it all look like? Try filling a page. Then give the page a title that encapsulates this section of writing.

2. **Where am I now?** Write down three or four feeling words that best describe your current state of mind and heart. Write more after reading and rereading what you wrote.

3. **Where do you want to go?** Write your intention. What do you want to heal? How do you want to change your relationship with your addicted loved one?

The next chapter will take you deeper into the rewrite of your family addiction story. You are becoming the creator of change, the one who can shift the paradigm from addiction to healing. Keep on and keep steady. Coming to terms with your place in all the messiness is just around the bend.

Subtle Footsteps

When use creates **PAIN**,
it's ADDICTION

Coming to Terms

Most assuredly your loved one's consequences will
continue to increase in both frequency
and magnitude until they
reach a point beyond the family's
ability or willingness to solve them.

❖   Ed Hughes, MPS, LICDC, Ronald Turner, M.D., CDCA,
Baffled by Addiction? Successful Strategies to Help Your Addicted Loved One

No one plans to plunge headlong into addiction. It comes unbidden.
Your loved one chose to begin drinking at age 16, eat Percocets at her
roommate's urging, snort cocaine at the mortgage bankers convention,
or shoot heroin "just this once," but did not envision surrendering her
life to drugs or alcohol. He could not imagine sitting drunk in a bar in
New Mexico, forgetting the promise he made to fly home in time for

his son's tenth birthday party in Indiana. The loving and devoted aunt could not imagine being uninvited to her favorite niece's high school graduation because she had shown up at baccalaureate giggly and high. The son who tried drugs or alcohol on a dare could not have imagined a level of desperation that would create a need to steal his dying mother's pain medication.

Addiction enters with silent, subtle footsteps, but once it grabs hold of a brain and body, it quickly becomes the built-in automatic fix-it place. The flood of pleasure elicited by an addict's use of alcohol or other drugs becomes the answer to all stressors and the easiest way to deal with all inner and outer problems. So why wouldn't he become a bit fussy, anxious, and edgy at the thought of stopping all use?

I'll never forget a young female client who was two weeks clean and struggling with her addiction to heroin. She sat in my office, checking out the framed credentials and licensures hanging on the wall. She looked at me head-on and asked, "Have you ever used heroin?"

Clients are often curious about whether their counselor has an addictive past and will often ask. I usually hedge the question by gently focusing them back on themselves. But for some reason, I felt compelled to answer.

"No," I said. "I've never used heroin."

"Then you don't know what the f…. you're talking about."

She had me there. Addiction can't be truly known by someone standing outside that brain chemistry. We can feel that twist in our heart space while someone we love becomes more deeply involved with drugs or alcohol, but we cannot know the scale or degree of that pull of chemistry. I imagine her brain felt naked and afraid without its familiar euphoric hiding place.

"I want to run," she said. "Heroin is my best friend."

"And your best enemy," I replied.

She wasn't truly in denial, but she was standing smack dab in the middle of her fear of living without her drug(s). Addictive use of substances slices healthy coping skills to pieces and addicts lose their ability to handle stress or the negative emotions connected to stress.

The young female client had become accustomed to burying all things negative through use of substances. But she was raw and honest.

"I don't know how to live sober," she said and began to cry. She was, at last, being real. Now our work could begin.

What is denial?

An addict's denial is difficult to understand. Why can't your son see his use of alcohol is strangling the meaning and purpose of his life? Why oh why can't your daughter stop her use of opiates long enough to see how much pain is being created by her use? Why can't your husband understand how much his drinking hurts you and his children? Why? Why? Why?

Try to understand it this way: the addict's denial of issues is a way of staying put. An addict's brain sits in a jail created by his brain chemistry, and the denial is the equivalent of three hots and a cot for that foggy brain. When he stops long enough to look around, he'll feel the entrapment, the fear, the pain of loss. So he doesn't stop. He doesn't look around for long. He just keeps on altering his chemistry, and he avoids the pain. The mood alteration offered by substances trumps reality. As wild and out of control as his life might look to family members watching from the sidelines, his brain chemistry remains awash in pleasure.

Think of sitting in your 2016 Chevy Malibu along a roadside during a blinding rainstorm. The windows fog over, but you feel safer inside the vehicle than outside. Drugs or alcohol have become your loved one's Chevy Malibu, his protection against the storms of life.

Your loved one will deny he's addicted and laugh off or explain away any concerns that spill from your well-intentioned mouth. Your brother may admit to "a few difficult nights," but claims with much bravado that he's in control of his use and is capable of stopping at any time. Just not yet.

The one addicted will try cutting back, switching drugs, or tossing out hard liquor while increasing his beer intake. People with an addiction to substances want to float on the chemical high and live without consequences. And they will try and try and try again, denying the need for change for as long as possible.

How about your denial?

Denial is as potent as any drug; we humans can mask anything we aren't ready to face. We become experts at covering our troubles with a thousand other names. Adding to the charade, an addict may state boldly, "Yes, I'm an alcoholic." Or, "Yes, I'm addicted, but I also know what I'm doing so you can just back off." During those types of exchanges, you may feel a glimmer of hope. He is, after all, admitting he's addicted. And he's reassuring you that he's okay, and both you and the addict want to believe that.

But you may as well try believing the Dutch folktale of a young boy who saves his entire village by plugging a hole in the dike with just one finger. A folktale is a story. The user's words are a story, one he's creating so he doesn't have to do the hard work of recovery.

Excusing the addict's raw and embarrassing behaviors is often more comfortable for you than staying with the emotions connected to what you are seeing. Andrea may have drunk too much at her high school reunion, to the point of falling onto the dessert table and wearing pecan pie bars down the front of her Ann Taylor blouse. Or she may have made sexual remarks to a classmate's spouse. But isn't that just Andrea when she has too much to drink? After all, nobody behaves well while intoxicated. So you blush over her behavior and try to forget the promise she made to you the night before the reunion to stop after two drinks.

"I think you'd better mind your drinking manners tomorrow night," you said.

"No problem. I know my limits. Two drinks, no more," said Andrea, and hugged you to seal the deal.

Perhaps your marriage seems otherwise healthy, but your husband's drinking habit almost always creates fear and tension between you and others. He made a pass at your sister on New Year's Eve. You cried the next morning while he held his head in his hands and apologized for what he remembered about last night's party. He leaned in closer and wanted to hug you. He claimed the beer he drank was craft beer, higher in alcohol content, and that he "finally" learned his lesson. You told him how humiliated you felt.

He acted sheepishly, and promised he'd stop all drinking "if that's what will make you happy." But that's also what he promised after he stumbled drunk into last year's family Easter gathering. And now you recall all the signs over the years and feel another layer of your denial peel away. Nothing you have said or done over time has quieted his obsession; his use of alcohol has continued to grow, as have his apologies, excuses, and reasons to drink. Things are becoming harder to justify, deny, or push to the side.

Your confusion, anger, and rattled psyche beg for answers, for ways to fix the problems. You just want to help. You think you can talk some sense into the addict. You give your son a verbal tongue-lashing and a list of "shoulds."

"You should be ashamed. You should stop hanging around with so-and-so. You should get a better job. You should stop lying to me. You should grow up, act your age, get a grip, stop acting like a criminal, get a better job, go live with your grandma."

Blah. Blah. Blah. "Shoulds" will always fall on an addict's deaf ears.

You find needles taped to the underside of bathroom cupboards, bottles of wine hidden in the toilet tank, or a stash of pills cuddled up next to the battery charger on the top shelf in the garage. Your love for your spouse, your brother, your mother, your sister, your son, your fiancé, or your daughter becomes muddled and muddied. The person you once knew and trusted has become extraordinarily untrustworthy.

But he does show up occasionally, claiming to be much better, so it's easy to drift in and out of denial. Some users try proving to themselves and others that they have not lost control. Your son will stop drinking for a week or two. Your daughter will prove to you she remains in control by staying away from opiates for a short while. You may even witness the trembles and shakes of her withdrawal and feel

27

enormous relief that the drugs are gone. You begin to believe she has turned the corner. But has she?

Who wants to face the reality of addiction? The one addicted doesn't, nor do you. Just as the addictive mind plays tricks on the one addicted, your thinking wobbles, and you will hesitate to call addiction what it is, despite the mounting evidence that your daughter's life has become severely impacted by her dependence on various types of substances. You vacillate and become less and less self-actuated and more and more reactive.

Raised in the house that Jack's alcoholism built, I learned the rules of addiction early and well: hide your embarrassment, be ashamed, be good, be quiet, be convincing, and don't rock the boat, particularly the addict's makeshift dinghy. Emotional patterning in my childhood had included two extremes; either stay numb or scream a lot in private.

I had absorbed much from living with my father's alcoholism. Little did I know that my psyche was deeply imprinted by the illness of our household and that when I married my high school sweetheart at age 19, the alcoholic lineage would continue.

I thought my husband-to-be was not at all like my father. He was, after all, a tender-hearted, Mensa-smart, George Clooney-handsome man, who had grown up in a wealthy everything-looked-good kind of family. But just because his mother wore furs and set their table with fine china and crystal, creating a prettier dining experience than my blue-collar family's Formica-top table, his family dynamics were similar. His mother was an alcoholic, so his baggage was as heavy as mine, and like a slow-footed monster, my young husband's drinking would plod towards the illness I so feared.

It took about eighteen years for his drinking to manifest as alcoholism. As his integrity became more compromised by his relationship with alcohol, I did more than my share of counting drinks, extracting promises, searching for bottles, crying, trembling, pleading: "If you loved me you would stop."

My missteps were many. I became judge and jury, leaving all love and warmth on the curb of our marriage while standing on my moral high ground. I despised the pain but didn't know how to share what

I was going through with anyone beyond our walls. Enveloped in the darkness of family addiction, I did not know how to remove the microscope from my husband. I held the pain tight to my chest, and I remained silent.

My husband's drinking didn't stop, but he did drink less at home. And there were periods where his drinking continued but without sloppy incidents. All the while, though, he was growing more and more physically and psychologically dependent on alcohol, and I made all the typical co-dependent mistakes as I tried to come to grips with the fact that I could not change him.

There I stood, front and center in my alcoholic marriage, with tons of unhealed emotional debris blinding my ability to see. This time, it wasn't my father's alcoholism; it was my husband's. And I was no longer a child; I was a strong, educated woman. But I couldn't see what I couldn't see. The rules of addiction do not change from generation to generation, so as I could not stop my father, I also couldn't stop my husband from drinking our marriage and our family into a sinkhole. But I would eventually learn how to shovel my codependency onto higher ground.

Shelley's story

"When I first witnessed my husband's growing alcohol problem, I was in complete disbelief. We were newlyweds. Both of us were professionals. Before I understood addiction, I thought I could make him stop drinking. I paid off his $12,000 credit card debt he had hidden from me because surely that would reduce his stress and give him less reason to drink. I went out of my way to do nice things, because then surely he wouldn't be so depressed and feel like he needed to drink. It was a back and forth pendulum swing. I would be overly nice until I would find him drunk again. Then I felt angry and frustrated. Nothing changed in our dynamic until I found help for myself."

What is an addiction? What is an addict's story?

Every addict's story carries a certain amount of uniqueness, but the similarities build the longer he or she remains in active addiction. Bank accounts (theirs and yours) are drained, jobs are lost, (theirs and maybe yours because of all the missed days you spend trying to clean up the addict's life). Arrests happen. Jail time is served. Families break down and break up. Lies are told. Lies are uncovered, and still the addict continues to use. So what is an addict's real story? How hard is it for an addict to stop? Is addiction a disease or a mental illness? Can it be diagnosed and defined? Shoring up your information about addiction can help you see the addict's deep challenges and recognize how closely your story has become connected to theirs. If you browse online, in books, attend A.A. or Al-Anon, or have sessions with a therapist, you will find varying viewpoints and opinions. And, yes, some therapists may deal with addiction in diverse ways and from a variety of perspectives.

In 1956, the American Medical Association began referring to alcoholism as a disease because it fit disease criteria: chronic, progressive and treatable, but fatal if left untreated. Alcoholics Anonymous, Al-Anon, and Narcotics Anonymous also have adopted the disease model.

In 2011, The American Society of Addiction Medicine (ASAM), a national professional society of physicians who work with the treatment and prevention of addiction, released their new definition. They renamed it a chronic brain disorder: "At its core, addiction isn't just a social problem or a moral problem or a criminal problem. It's a brain problem," said Dr. Michael Miller, past president of ASAM.

In 2013, the National Institute on Drug Abuse updated The Diagnostic and Statistical Manual of Mental Disorders DSM-5, the manual used by clinicians to diagnose mental disorders. The authors no longer differentiated between substance abuse and dependency. The DSM-5 now places problematic use in a single category: substance use disorder. Definitions can vary, but it isn't necessary to quarrel over definition or verbiage. You can pick the terminology that works best for you and move forward. You already know that whatever you call it, addiction is debilitating, and creates much collateral damage.

After 30 plus years of working as a Licensed Independent Chemical Dependency Counselor, I subscribe to the disease/illness perspective, viewing both alcoholism and addiction to other drugs as a brain-related illness. The trademark of addiction is that the brain's chemistry becomes compromised, and consequently, so does the addict's ability to make rational decisions, which leads, in turn, to a compromised value system and big-time pain.

Questions remain about the relationship of childhood trauma to one's development of a substance use disorder. Is an alcoholic's drinking pattern connected to a severe lacking in her childhood? Substances can create an emotional buffer, wrapping cotton around a user's need to heal wounds, easing the hurts that preceded drug or alcohol use. So yes, sometimes drinking patterns can become connected to a user's need to dull emotional pain, but it's also important to remember that addiction is, in the end, a separate diagnosis.

Addiction often overlaps other mental disorders, which can complicate treatment. If your loved one has been the victim of childhood trauma or has a history of other psychiatric illnesses, it's important for those not to be overlooked. But it's not your job to tease apart other illnesses from a substance use disorder. That job belongs to a professional—a trained clinician who will know all the appropriate questions to ask during the intake and evaluation process if and when your addicted loved one decides to seek professional help.

It's the clinician's job to obtain the fullest view possible of the addict during the intake process. The psychologist, nurse practitioner, psychiatrist, social worker or chemical dependency counselor, or whoever winds up in the driver's seat of the addict's treatment plan, will gather data not only about substance use history but will also collect information about family history, childhood upbringing, history of trauma, depression, and other mood disorder symptoms.

You could be an asset to the clinician doing the intake only if your loved one gives written permission for you to be present and included. It's also important not to blame the addiction on other disorders and not to blame any other diagnosed illness for the development of addiction. They are separate but related, and neither will benefit from blame. All levels of illness diagnosed during the assessment process need treatment, but the clinician should draw up the appropriate treatment plan.

Depression almost always accompanies addiction, or it may have preceded the use of substances. The sufferings of active addiction—compromised values, job loss, relationship neglect, and loss of familial or friendship support—do register somewhere deep inside the addict and will fuel an already low mood state. Brain chemistry shifts dramatically during active addiction, jeopardizing the brain's ability to sustain healthy levels of vital neurotransmitters, the brain's own "feel-good" chemicals.

It's difficult even for experts to know whether depression is related to use or was present before use. Furthermore, it's all but impossible to sort out other disorders while the addict is still using. If depression becomes the focus without treating addiction, not much will improve in your user's life. Co-occurring disorders may overlap, but they are not the same. Both require treatment for recovery to be successful.

Addiction takes place in the brain's reward center; the portion of the brain meant to maximize pleasure and minimize pain. Non-addicts have a filtering system that offers sane messages regarding the use of mind-altering substances. "I've had enough. Better call a taxi." "I have work tomorrow, so a shot of tequila will have to wait." "Heroin? That can kill me. No way."

In full-blown addiction, all filters are gone. The brain becomes enamored of the high of chemical pleasure-beyond-measure. An addict will seek that pleasure without considering potential consequences: "My wife will be angry." "I'm spending my rent money on opiates." "I need to be at my mother's funeral this afternoon." A compulsive need overpowers rational thinking, and the drive for the high takes control.

Feeding that compulsion becomes a fundamental need for the addict; getting drunk or high prevails over all else. Love, work, and anything associated with life's deep meaning, become secondary. *You* become secondary. The brain's five thought processes that keep the addict on life's healthy track—logic, judgment, prediction, calculation, and decision making—are buried beneath his or her unhealthy relationship with drugs and alcohol.

Addiction is *the physical adaptation of the reward pathways of the brain to the presence of a certain mix of chemicals.* Dopamine and serotonin, the feel-good neurotransmitters, become significantly enhanced as alcohol and illicit drugs cross the blood-brain barrier. Stopping use produces a halt to the chemical rush, and the brain feels both empty and deprived. Essentially, the brain becomes a fit-throwing toddler, pounding its fists. It wants what it wants when it wants it. A crash occurs, withdrawal ensues, and the addict sits in misery or, at the least, substantial physical discomfort. Using their favorite substance will assuage the chemically depleted brain; it will offer a numbing peace, take away guilt, and create a reprieve. That's highly seductive.

An addict's story

"My name is Anna. I had my first drink at age 13. The alcohol came from my parent's liquor cabinet. I was sexually molested for several years, beginning at age 6. I never told my parents, and by the time I turned 13, I felt like a loser, a super dirty, horrible person. The alcohol from that cabinet numbed those feelings.

"I didn't drink every day but would find the adult's liquor cabinet when I babysat kids. I would drink enough to get a buzz on, but not so much the parents would notice when they came home. I just didn't think it was a problem. One of my first consequences happened in high school when I got drunk at a wedding reception. I remember how people looked at me. I felt like they were looking down on me. Another time I busted up my knee and had to tell my parents a lie. I couldn't tell them I was drunk and fell down.

"My blackouts began when I was 16. I didn't know that's what they were called. I thought the word meant passing out and I never passed out from drinking. I just couldn't remember things the next day. Although bad things happened to me when I was drunk, I didn't believe the problem was alcohol. I thought my problem was that I just couldn't stand myself. My drinking was easy to hide because I was a binge drinker. I didn't drink every day, so it was easier for me to convince myself that all was well enough. Looking back, I see that my drinking was a slow form of suicide.

"*I moved away from my parents' house early, so they didn't know how much or how often I was drinking. I spent time with people who accepted me and who didn't challenge my growing attachment to alcohol. I married at age 19, but I wanted to spend more time with alcohol than with him, so I left that marriage.*

"*My second marriage lasted five years, and he was an alcoholic. He was wealthy, and he was highly controlling and physically abusive. My drinking and my self-esteem became much worse during that marriage. I somehow found the courage to leave him, but my drinking continued to worsen.*

"*I moved back in with my parents, and they began realizing my drinking was out of control. They threw out all the alcohol in the house. I was pissed. I was an adult and thought they were treating me like a child. I still found a way to drink. I got into another relationship, and things got worse. I tried to commit suicide.*

"*One night, in 2005, I was in a car with the man who would become my husband. Both of us were intoxicated. I don't remember to this day, who was driving because I was in a blackout. We were involved in a bad car accident. He was severely injured and spent nine months in a hospital. I ended up having 300 stitches in my head.*

"*I still thought my drinking was normal, that I just had bad luck when I drank. After the accident, my attorney recommended I have an alcohol assessment. I remember sitting across from the desk from a clinician at the treatment facility, telling her I was only there because my attorney said it would help my court case. The clinician was both kind and direct. She diagnosed me with alcoholism.*

"*My way of drinking was called something? Wasn't I just a bad person? My drinking habits could now be called a treatable illness? I felt a huge sense of relief at the diagnosis.*

"*I completed intensive outpatient treatment and worked on my treatment plan as assigned by my counselor. I learned about my past, and how to deal with my feelings. I learned how to separate my rational thinking from my drunk thinking, and how to control my "stinking thinking." I was taught that my self-esteem was up to me, and was not up to what others thought of me. I learned that I could develop my own concept of God/Higher Power. I attended A.A. regularly and found a home group.*

"*I have not had a drink since 2005.*"

It's hard to predict how long Anna's addiction to alcohol would have continued if the accident had not happened. It served as the jolt needed to penetrate her denial and become ready to heal both her alcoholism and the wounds beneath.

Examining your role

Coming to terms with family addiction is not an easy thing to do. For years you may have tried your best not to see what you see. You may have bailed out, lectured, given advice, gotten angry, and created soft psychological and physical places for the addict to fall because you didn't know how not to. Rescuing became the norm, allowing you to feel more in control and perhaps a little less desperate. It gave you something to do, but it also kept you from getting in touch with your own needs. Focusing on how to make the addict's life better became your way of surviving, but it also kept you smack-dab in the middle of the insidious web of addiction and tied to the dysfunction of the one addicted.

Carolyn's story

"It was easy for me to rationalize my daughter's addiction. At first, I chalked up her odd behavior to that of a moody teenager. Then, when the drugs showed up at the house, I believed any feasible explanation she provided. She wasn't using the drugs; she was just holding them for someone else; the girl sitting next to her put them in her purse when she wasn't looking; and so on. I firmly believed that there was no way my daughter could be an addict. And since she didn't seem like the down-and-out-addicts I knew from my professional life, I was positive that what I was dealing with was something (really, anything) else.

Perhaps you have become a helicopter parent, hovering over your addicted daughter, aiming to learn all you can about her using patterns. You chastise and plead, and she becomes better at hiding her use. You haul her to an A.A. or N.A. meeting, strongly suggest she change jobs or stay away from friends who use. She attends the meetings but continues to spend time with using friends. You change the locks on your doors after she steals your grandmother's jewelry. You tell her she's not welcome in your house as long as she's using, and you assume that will make a difference. But it doesn't. She keeps on using, so you do what you can to keep her life intact, basing your decisions on genuine love, care, and concern. You cry, she promises to do better, the cycle continues, and the circle tightens. Thoughts and behaviors conducive to health disappear, and her life unravels before your eyes.

You remain focused on fixing her or on repairing the damage created by addiction. Beneath all those attempts spins the real truth: **You and all the love you have shown the addict have become a part of the problem, and the best solution is for you to learn more about how to do less.**

Once you learn more about your place in family addiction and your codependent role becomes more evident, you can begin to work on yourself rather than on the addict. Pulling yourself out of the all-consuming patterns created by addiction is not just an idea, it's a choice, and the power of choice belongs to you and you alone. It's a hard alternative, and you must keep in mind that dragging yourself away from unhealthy behavior patterns is not just a one-time decision, it's a series of decisions best made a day at a time. We change bit by bit. We get there, little by little. So be patient with yourself as you learn and grow.

You are as hopeless as Don Quixote fighting imaginary windmills if you think you can tame someone's addictive, compulsive drive for substance use. You can never become wise enough or learned enough to outthink or outsmart a loved one who is bent on continuing their use of substances. You can't be mean enough or loud enough. As long as addiction remains in high gear, the one addicted will find a way to use. But as you gather facts, as you speak in-depth to others who have recovery knowledge, you'll find the dynamics harder to ignore.

Saying you can't cure your loved one is not the same as saying you have no power. You take your power back when you tell the addict the truth about what you see. You become the writer of your recovery script when you share with your sister how her drunken behavior affects you and set limits on when, or if, you spend time with her if she is high or intoxicated. When you shock your son by saying "No" to yet another request for a loan, you are exercising your recovery muscle.

Because addiction is unreasonable and unsound, it may feel like a slippery slope for you when you begin setting those limits. Turning down his request for money, housing, school tuition or transportation to a dealer's house when your addicted son claims he will die if "you make me go through heroin withdrawal" is frightening. You are trying out new behaviors that will eventually redefine your role with your addicted loved one, but all that newness can feel off-putting. Just don't forget what the truth is: you aren't *making* your son go through withdrawal. You are asking him to accept responsibility for his addiction. Withdrawal is a necessary evil.

Remember the addict has to play mind games to maintain his dependency, and while you remain inside all the unhealed psychology of addiction, you will have difficulty thinking clearly because your emotions are leading the way. Emotions play a role in all relationships but allowing them the starring role in dramas connected to your addicted loved one will produce nothing but more chaos and more drama.

When you begin facing the facts of addiction, you probably will feel guilt and fear during the education and detachment processes. But the illness has nothing to do with you, so don't make it about yourself. Your daughter's choice to continue using substances may feel like a personal attack, but it's not. She's craving a drug or a drink and is not thinking about hurting you. Her use of substances is a means to an end: swallow a handful of pills, drink a pint of vodka, inject heroin into a vein, and the mental and physical discomfort ends and calm enters. And yes, it's a dangerous illness.

More truth

Addiction to alcohol or other drugs is a physiological illness occurring inside the addict's brain and body and has zip-zero-nothing to do with you. A mother mistakenly believes her 25 year-old daughter's daily heroin habit is connected to parental neglect: "She uses because her father left us when she was 10." A father bleeds hope and money into his 30-year-old son's addiction to Percocet: "He just needs something to relieve stress while he's finishing his law degree." A husband remains bent on saving his Harvard graduate wife from her love affair with Grey Goose: "She's still mourning her mother's death."

But listen up: addiction is not created by a father who neglects or a mother who dies. When a breathalyzer registers .32 for the 34-year-old Harvard graduate, it's due to her cellular adaptation to alcohol. She may have begun her slide into drinking through the channel of grief, but her daily and excessive drinking and the bevy of consequences connected to her drinking are symptoms of her addiction to alcohol. And that is not the mother's fault or even the graduate's fault for that matter. It is what it is.

The pleasure center of her brain has developed a growing need for the sensation obtained from drugs or alcohol, and the need cannot be removed by your wishing it away. The talons of addiction sink deep, lifting from your son's brain his ability to keep promises and replacing all that's good and predictable with sheer craziness. That's the makeup of addiction.

But what if it isn't?

Perhaps you're still not sure your loved one is addicted. Most of us do our share of rationalizing, of explaining away all out-of-control use before we admit that addiction is alive and well inside our loved one's body and mind. The word "addiction" carries with it such dark stereotypes: addicts live under bridges and in alleys, swig from bottles wrapped in brown bags, and are the dregs of society.

But the truth is that addicted people come in all shapes and sizes. They are CEO's of large companies, homemakers, students, grandfathers, grandmothers, teachers, professors, philosophers, artists, writers, dancers, attorneys, judges, politicians, police officers, priests, nuns, child-care workers, actors, ministers, movie stars, soccer moms, and fathers who coach. Addiction does not pick and choose; it can capture anyone.

While it's not your job to officially diagnose your loved one, it's important for you to come to terms with your need to change *yourself* in the face of the addict's using behavior. You can begin this process by taking a close look at how your life has been impacted emotionally, financially, spiritually, and physically by the consequences of their continued use of substances. Growth is enhanced when you are witness to how vain your attempts have been in stopping the landslide of addiction. Despite your lectures, he's still getting high.

If it's full-blown addiction, you are not as important to your loved one as the drug or drink, and that truth does not in any way equate to the addiction being your fault. Your view of your loved one as a person suffering from an illness *that is not her fault but is her responsibility* will allow you to stand more firmly in your own recovery process.

You will continue to have questions. Seriously, is it him? Is it me? Am I too cranky, too judgmental, too demanding, too emotional, too uppity, too rigid, too extroverted, too introverted, too educated, too uneducated, too controlling, too passive, too rich, too poor, too fearful, too numb? It's possible that you are a little bit of some of those, but that still doesn't make YOU the reason for your loved one's addiction. You must begin to define and separate your issues from the addict's problems. So please grab the hand of someone who knows more than you about families and addiction and ask for help. Find a therapist who specializes in working with families of addicts or a friend who has made a successful attempt at the setting of firm and loving boundaries with their addict.

The closer you have become tied to the addict, the more likely you have been asked many times to act as a go-to problem solver. As addiction builds in magnitude and intensity, the opportunities to rescue your addicted loved one will also grow.

You can and must do less to help the addict stand upright in her life, both literally and figuratively. Surround yourself with people who can help guide your mind toward healing, your spirit toward peace, and the addict toward accountability.

* * * * *

Story Pages

Answering the questions at the close of Chapter One helped to focus your intention. The answers bear witness to the parts of your life crying out for attention. Acknowledging how tightly bound you've become to the negativity born of a loved one's addiction cuts a new pathway, a place to broaden your vision and create new and healthier choices.

Continuing to deepen your knowledge about addiction is all-important. The more you learn, the easier it is to remove yourself from that problem-solver role. Your goal is to hold the addict accountable and to become aligned with your support system. Becoming educated about the full impact of addiction on family members will help you come to terms with changes you need to make to detach from the craziness that always accompanies active addiction.

Your second Story Page: Grab your journal, legal pad or iPad, tablet or computer.

What were the "aha" moments in this chapter? What information did you find helpful? What are you *feeling* after reading the information presented in this chapter? What does the "coming-to-terms" process mean to you?

Now make a couple of lists:

List #1: Number a page from one to ten and write down ten times you have caught your addict/alcoholic in a lie in the past six months.
List #2: Identify ten ways you have tried to stop or control your addict's use of substances in the past six months or year.

The next chapter further defines the feelings and behaviors of codependency. You will continue to learn how to claim your healing, how to strengthen your resolve to learn a new framework for loving, and how to reshape your relationship with all parts of family addiction.

Codependent Attachment

...the lifespan of any particular
emotion is only one and a half minutes. After that, we have
to revive the emotion and get it going again. Our usual process
is that we automatically do revive it by feeding it with an internal
conversation about how another person is
the source of our discomfort.

❖ Pema Chodron, *Taking the Leap, Freeing
Ourselves from Old Habits and Fears*

Relationships are where we live, love and learn. Relationships are where
we are called into growth. It's not difficult to stay calm and content
while sitting alone in a small cabin surrounded by the quiet of tall pine
trees. The blue sky overhead, the sound of a gurgling brook at the
bottom of the hill. Just you, the trees, the trill of birds. But let's face

it, put another human being in that setting with you and the dynamics change. Put addiction in that cabin with you and it'll blow off the relational roof.

Healthy love relationships need to be explored before we consider the outlier referred to as codependency. Merriam-Webster has much to say about love. Here are but a few references: "strong affection, an attraction based on sexual desire, affection based on admiration, warm attachment, unselfish loyalty and benevolent concern for the good of the other." What the dictionary doesn't mention is how much compromise is needed. We may recognize the feeling of love but may not understand how to do the work of love.

Romantic love will fail unless lovers learn how to accept the good and not so good about each other. You meet someone and feel the pull of chemistry and magnetism. Sigh. You feel excited about creating a life together. Sigh. He moves in. Sigh.

But at some point, the learning will begin. For starters, he leaves the toilet seat up. You hate that. She leaves her make-up strewn across the bathroom counter, and that annoys you. Even if you commit to staying healthy in that loving partnership, even if both of you pledge to remain honest, to listen and to honor the integrity of the other, most people don't become champions without practice. We can become irate and feel humbled by a mate who calls us out.

"You are stubborn and selfish," says the one.

"And you whine when you don't get your way," says the other.

So that's love? The kind described in the dictionary? The kind we hear about in songs?

Now let's talk about babies and parental love. The creative and dreamy time of pregnancy and baby showers, so full of joy and celebration. Then the birth experience and love at first sight for the tiny wiggly one. Next comes the crying jags, sleepless nights, sore breasts if you're a nursing mother, diapers that smell like rotting roadkill, clothes covered in spit-up, ear infections, coughing and tiny clogged nasal passages. You feel the exhaustion of being a new parent and wonder if you'll be able to handle the "work" of love. But somehow you grow into the role you've chosen, and you slowly learn the requirements of love. Love is more than a just a feeling. It taps every vulnerable button, turns your heart into a school where you learn about yourself and all those others. Love is multi-faceted, multi-layered, and comes laden with responsibility.

And along comes your loved one's addiction

Throughout the previous chapter, I've referred to codependency without offering a full definition. The term has been around for forty plus years and remains the central theme in families suffering from addiction. The term codependency has evolved through the decades, beginning as an expression in the late 1970s and referring to traits and repetitive behaviors among families of alcoholics. The word took on a life of its own and by the 1980s was applied not only to families of addicts/alcoholics but also to families headed by abusive, neglectful parents.

Although there is a great deal of literature linking codependency to trauma and family dysfunction, for this book I'm connecting the term only with families of alcoholics and addicts. All the references and explanations regarding family dysfunction or codependency spring from the seedbed of addiction.

Family members of alcoholics were first referred to as co-alcoholics. I remember bristling at that reference when beginning my recovery journey. I felt it linked me too tightly with problems that belonged to my alcoholics. After all, the dysfunction wasn't mine. They were creating the messes, not me. So how could I possibly be co-anything? Co-alcoholic? Wasn't I the victim in the drama created by addiction? I felt defensive, blameful, full of false pride, and like a member of the walking wounded.

Despite my protests and my feelings of contempt for the term co-alcoholic, I continued to look at how my life had become governed by the pain connected to the behavior of my addicted loved ones. And finally accepted that yes, the term fits me like a well-worn glove. Co-alcoholic.

It fit because the term referred to those who tried managing the alcoholic and yes, that was me. It fit because it related to the feelings and behaviors of those who wanted to control an illness that is uncontrollable by anyone except the one addicted. It included those family members who remained highly reactive to a loved one's use of alcohol or drugs and had developed strategies to deny the need to begin healing themselves. I realized that the label referred to me and those parts of me imprisoned by fear. What if my father drank again? What if my husband was indeed an alcoholic? What did that say about me? What would others think of my family or me as a whole? All that pain kept secret, hidden under the guise of "me" and "my." I was making someone else's illness all about me.

I was all those names: codependent, co-addict, and co-alcoholic. I often felt besotted with my fears and anxieties, unable to make clear decisions about my life independent of the problems created by relationships with active alcoholics. I was failing at making any lasting difference in their lives and most important, I was close to drowning in my own.

The birth of codependency

The breeding ground for codependency can be a broad and deep oasis. If you were raised in a home steeped in parental addiction, you are likely to grow into adulthood with unmet emotional needs. You are also likely to have love affairs or marriages with alcoholics/addicts; the patterning seems lodged in your psychological makeup. Like it or not, codependents tend to find addicts and alcoholics to love and cherish, which can add layers to a healing process. It did to mine. Looking back, I see I had a double dose of codependency to heal. The first layer was connected to my father's alcoholism; the second layer was from my marriage to a man who developed alcoholism. The codependency spoken of in this book is primarily connected to you as an adult dealing with the emotions and behaviors of a current loved one's addiction. If your addictive story has generational roots, the information and exercises found here can also help you begin unpacking those older layers.

Remember it is the fear that sits so squarely in your heart space that gives you reasons to cover up, change, or fix the substance user's circumstances. Remember that the addict's other desires become secondary to getting high or drunk, so as a good codependent, you develop out-of-control anxiety. You take on far more than belongs to you. Why wouldn't you? During the insanity created by addiction, love and protection go into overdrive and your health—mental, physical, emotional, and spiritual—takes a back seat. Your needs become subsumed by the pathological desires of the addict. Loving a daughter, son, spouse, partner, or friend while they are under the pull and influence of addiction is a journey like no other. It begins to feel a bit like walking through a field of emotional landmines; another crisis is always just around the corner. You can expect one blow up after another until you find another way to navigate.

Codependent symptoms are not built all at once. If your loved one's addiction to substances begins as a crawl, taking years to develop consistent symptoms, your responses may crawl as well. Your symptoms heighten as the days, months, or years of negative consequences roll through your life. To see more clearly where you stand in the addict's life, you need to begin identifying your codependent traits. Read the list below and select the characteristics that apply to you and to the relationship you share with your addicted loved one:

- Your emotional world seems scripted by someone else's behavior
- Your emotional responses toward an addicted loved one's behavior are often patterned, explosive, reactionary. (So much anger, sadness, resentment)
- Critical areas of your life are negatively affected by your strong reactions, and your life burns brightly only between crises created by someone else's substance use
- When you see yet another crisis heading the addict's way, both your head and heart kick into high gear. You feel that toxic mix of fear, anxiety, shame, and anger

- Your fix-it list is a foot long
- You call him in sick, so the boss won't think he's just blown off another day
- You put money into your sister's account so she can pay the rent and not bounce yet another check
- You tell the coach your son's dirty drug test came from a few pain pills you gave him from your prescription to help him deal with the injury he supposedly incurred the day before the screen

You can barely keep track of all the lies you tell to protect your loved one. And your lies may keep the wolves from the addict's door for a short while. But those lies will never rectify or heal addiction. And yes, you are as hooked on your son as he is on drugs. You have become ensnared in the discord of addiction, and your profile now looks similar to an addict's. As the addicted loved one develops a high tolerance for a substance, you develop a high tolerance for negative behaviors. Your husband lies about his use, and you tell tales to his coworkers, your friends, even other family members, about how well things are going.

The emotional craziness of codependency contorts your thinking and impacts all parts of your life. Like a hamster running on a wheel, you spin in the circle of worry: crying, begging and pleading as you run side by side with the addict. The next day or next week produces more of the same because your daughter is still using heroin or your husband is still drinking, and you remain confounded by the mounting risks, losses, lies, and cover-ups. Without ever picking up a drug or drink, you develop symptoms similar to an addict. You're co-addicted and codependent. Your relationship becomes toxic for both you and the addict. You are unhealthy for one another. Your behavior is as loopy as the one addicted to substances. He won't stop using, and you refuse to let go.

Remember the addict remains in denial for as long as possible and will do whatever is needed to continue his use of substances. Your feelings have not disappeared from his mind or emotions, but they have become so buried by your husband's need for a drink or your daughter's urgent desire for a drug that you fall to the lower rung on the addict's ladder of relational needs. You watch as your loved one blows up his life, time after time.

A loved one caught in the throes of active addiction cannot put your needs first. Stop expecting it. An addict's strongest relationship is with his drug of choice, and his brain convinces him that all is well. Addiction has wounded his thinking processes, and his interests lay elsewhere.

It is important to recognize the need for change. You begin the process by taking an in-depth look at the misguided beliefs or hopes that keep you unhealthily hooked. What started as natural responses to the strange habits of addiction have evolved into codependency. And the caveat? Those familiar response patterns keep you from seeing or claiming your God-given right to peace of mind and heart. Codependency can smother all that is good in your life.

Exploring the truth—and depth—of your codependency will feel threatening and scary. You're being dragged out of your comfort zone. Dropping your son's hand and dealing with the fear of taking a stand against his addiction will likely bring about self-doubt. You may feel you're disloyal. He is, after all, your son, and it's counter-intuitive not to offer assistance while you watch his life hit the skids. It is difficult to find or maintain a loving balance while you ride the teeter-totter of someone else's destructive lifestyle.

Of course, you want to help. Healthier ways of supporting him will come, but not while you're walking in the quicksand of codependency. The addict will pull you under. Health will not happen for you until you find a steady place to stand, a place where you can begin to see just how screwed your life has become. Taking that look is difficult. It's also brave, crucial and necessary. And you'll need help.

Kathleen's story

"As an independent, motivated, relatively grounded woman, the word 'codependent' was foreign to me. It did not resonate on any level...until I learned my daughter was a heroin addict.

"Controlling her addiction became an obsession. I worried day and night and spent countless hours trying to figure out how to get things back to the way they used to be. I was a resourceful woman, and surely I could fix this. I just needed to find the right people to help her. The one thing I hadn't figured into this grand plan was my daughter's unwillingness to receive it.

"Over a two-year period, my daughter plunged deeper into her addiction, and there was nothing I could do to reverse it. My self-worth took a beating. How could I not solve this? A friend suggested I attend Al-Anon. I found fellow travelers, kind, open, insightful women who understood both my pain and my shame. I also joined a forward-thinking family support group and explored my unhealthy and unproductive behaviors with a therapist. I began to take care of me.

"Letting go and accepting were the two hardest recovery concepts for me to grasp as a codependent. By accepting my daughter's path as her own, I am now learning to let her life unfold without my intervention. My role is to merely love her. I have embraced the idea that I can (and do) set boundaries with her because that helps me stay serene and sane—not because I want to control or punish her.

"Fast forward to today…my daughter is in recovery, and I am grateful every day that she chooses to be sober. I've shared with her what I believe to be my contribution to her drug problem. She doesn't see it that way, but that doesn't matter. I witness her discovering who she is and it makes me incredibly proud."

Time to undo, not do, redo

To begin, you must realize that you have been held hostage by your emotions—and emotions are temporary. They are fleeting, but they can pack a punch. Anger, fear, and anxiety are three powerful emotions that will shove a codependent into wanting to DO something about the addict. These emotions have likely ruled your behaviors for some time. Your work now includes becoming more aware of what is happening in your heart space and finding ways to honor those feelings without jumping into the addict's place of turmoil.

A codependent's modus operandi is to hold feelings tight and recycle them through rumination and worry. When you ruminate about the addicted loved one, you create more anxiety, fear, resentment, and confusion. Your repetitive inner monologue—she will disgrace herself yet again, he can't go to jail one more time, what will my friends say, what did I do to deserve this, he may die, I didn't raise her to put a needle in her arm—clutters your mind. While you are recycling thoughts and feelings, you are refraining from cleaning up your emotional environment and accepting the challenges of change. Those emotions belong to you, not to the addict. You can honor negative feelings without spinning out. There's no need to allow them to put your life into a skid. Emotions should not become your overlord.

It is possible to feel angry at the addict and not act on it. It is possible to recognize how anxious you feel and take a walk or ride your bike or do yoga instead of sitting and chewing on negative feelings. It creates a healthy change for you when you acknowledge your fears and talk them out with another person in recovery or write them out on a legal pad, and then wad up the page and throw it into the trash. I'm not recommending that you stuff your feelings or numb them in any way. I'm asking you to explore other ways of honoring them without jumping into rescue behaviors or trying to be more than you are. You are not meant to play God, and you are not intended to heal your loved one's addiction. You are a witness, a bystander. But you will become a victim if you don't step out of the way.

Consider how many hours, days, months, and years you've spent ruminating about the addict in your life: her use, her reputation, his bank account, his unpredictable job losses, none of which you can control. All that time spent with those recurring feelings is a horrid way to outsource your energy and deplete your God-given time and talents. Recognizing how your emotions and internal conversations have been running your life is a huge but necessary realization if you are to change your dynamics.

Trying to untwist codependency from ordinary kindness is hard; it will take time, due time and "do" time. You must learn to do things differently. You must examine your emotional instincts and reactive behaviors; you must feel those strong pulls on your heart and psyche and resist them as you begin undoing your relational dynamics.

Look at those obsessive thoughts you drag around like a bag of rocks. The constant worrying and anxiety or relentless anger about the addict leave you feeling wrung out and exhausted. Do you ever experience moderate or severe depression or question your self-worth while watching your loved one suffer from his or her addictive choices? Yes, that can feel like love, but it carries so many codependent traits that you need to call them what they are.

Empathy, caring, and normal human concern is not the same as codependency. You will not stop suffering if your loved one continues to remain addicted. You will stay caring and concerned. The difference is you will not walk on the dark side with your alcoholic. Your life will be controlled by you, not by your loved one's illness. All change feels like a walk in the dark at first. That's why changing the way you respond to addiction requires such diligence. And courage, and all the outside support you can find.

The birth of Al-Anon

Lois Wilson founded the first support group for family members of alcoholics. She founded Al-Anon soon after her husband, Bill, co-founded Alcoholics Anonymous in 1935. Lois wanted to connect with others who were tired of suffering from their loved ones' illnesses. She had watched as Bill failed many attempts at maintaining sobriety, and she was fed up with suffering alone. Lois began holding meetings for wives of alcoholics. Together the women began developing tools to help themselves, to take their microscopes off the ones addicted to alcohol and focus instead on themselves. These courageous women started a movement of their own as they sat together and shared their stories. Sharing their experiences created spiritual, mental, and emotional strength to carry each of them along a path of healing. You will, as you continue to read on in this book, be invited over and over to find your way into circles of helpers. And there are many different kinds of circles; ask for help to discover yours.

Making the hard choices

As I mentioned in the last chapter, your loved one's addiction can happen slowly or it can explode with rapid-fire speed. Most alcoholics spend years controlling their use of alcohol just enough to remain functional in critical life areas, particularly in the field of employment. They can drink alcoholically on weekends for years and pull it together during the week. So you gradually develop response patterns as you witness your brother move in and out of functionality. Opiate addicts, on the other hand, develop dependency much more quickly, and life patterns are altered sooner, which brings along a different, more hurried set of complications.

If addiction happens quickly, it may seem impossible to believe. Before your daughter left for college, there were no apparent problems. Halfway through her sophomore year, your high school valedictorian is failing her college classes, not attending most of them, losing weight—and money is missing from your checking account. What on earth is happening?

Wasn't it just last month she was focused and excited about her studies, about completing her degree? You begin asking questions while sitting at the breakfast table one Wednesday morning and are shocked to learn your daughter started using opiates after a friend offered her an Adderall as a "study aid" the night before an English Lit exam. "I just wanted to get an A," she says.

She finally shares her story, tells you how quickly her use of Adderall led to her use of opiates, how fast her tolerance escalated, how expensive it became to maintain her opiate addiction and thus her reason for turning to heroin, which is "so much cheaper to maintain," she says. "I didn't mean for this to happen."

She confesses to you that she is "a junkie," and you are left holding onto nothing but fear, disbelief, shame, and anger. Your anger becomes focused on the friend who gave your daughter the Adderall, and you vow to do anything in your power to get your daughter clean.

But here's where the old parenting framework needs an overhaul.

The way you show love needs to change. What this new daughter, this addicted girl or woman, needs from you more than anything else, is for you to learn about addiction and the pressure it puts on family members to enable and rescue. She needs you to sort out her needs from your own, to begin healing yourself, and to find ways to hold her accountable for her own choices. It is not about the friend who gave her the Adderall. It is about your daughter's decision to take it.

Codependency is about you, not your loved one. It is your son's addiction to substances, not yours. It is your sister's decision to cop drugs, not yours. It is your husband's compulsion to drink in the morning before heading to work, not yours. The addict is living out the addict's story. You are living out the codependent tale, and you are its author. You may be able to have a positive impact on the user by changing the way you respond to the drama created by his use, but it is ultimately the addict who will decide to stop or continue substance use. Directing rage at your son when he picks up yet again after he promised to remain clean produces more drama and more pain. The fact remains: your addicted son will continue to let you down as long as he maintains active addiction. Remaining loyal to his needs and demands will only deepen your pain, smother your spirit, strangle your inner voice, and distort your ability to practice the behaviors of healthy love. There will be no winners.

The bottom line with codependency is that it exists to keep you away from those all-important inner truths. Codependent behaviors are, at their base, misguided attempts to make yourself feel better or help you not feel at all. Those behaviors keep the lions from your door and help you feel useful, but they also keep you from dealing with your inside story. You leave your spiritual self for a bit and travel to a La-La Land where wishes and dreams rule, where you lose your grip on what's real.

La-La Land

That may sound harsh to you. I was shocked, disheartened, and angry at myself when I learned that during my father's and ex-husband's drinking days my behaviors sprouted from La-La Land. The things I did during my pre-recovery days kept the sun from shining on my own screwed up inside story. My healing journey began when I accepted the need to deal with that screwed up inside story and to untangle my unhealthy emotional responses from the behavior of those addicted.

I learned that codependency could be deeply layered, multifaceted and emotionally messy. I learned what codependency was, but also what it was not.

Codependency is *not:*

- Clear, rational thinking
- Healthy response to the needs of another
- Character strength
- A way to improve sanity
- Ordained by God as a way to help the alcoholic become sober
- The safe way to proceed. It will not earn the addicted one a bed in rehab. It will not bring health and well-being to you or your loved one. It will not heal unresolved issues

Those unhealthy responses are bandages that cannot possibly cover the illness of addiction. Would you hand a band-aid to a loved one suffering from a broken leg? Of course not. Grabbing the bottle away from your son while raging at him when he shows up drunk at his mother's retirement party does not reflect health or healing. But it does reflect rage. Rage and other strong emotions can become quite toxic, creating malicious behaviors you will regret later. Your loved one has an illness, and the illness creates pain and embarrassment for you. That's what is real.

Codependent responses offer you a reprieve, but a bail-out is another one of those bandages, allowing you to hang onto the false belief that providing help for your family member will finally make the difference and make her want to get sober. Providing another month's rent will surely be the key. Taking a second job so you can help her buy a car will make such a positive difference. Despite the fact that she is still using, she claims to have "cut back."

You're still walking in the fantasy laid out by the addict. That's La-La Land. Wishes have never been horses; else your addict would have ridden out of fantasyland long ago.

Elizabeth's story

"After four years of health and sobriety, my husband relapsed with a vengeance. I had begun to take his sobriety for granted, convinced his recovery was total and would last forever...I was angry, not only because he was back to square one, but because for those four years of his recovery, I had so neglected my own. My purpose had been to help him be comfortable in his sobriety. I went into action; after all, I was an excellent enabler and codependent. I got him into treatment, researched the best places for outpatient treatment, and drove him there each day before I went to work to make sure he made it. All of my attempts were for nothing because later he hid vodka in his suitcase during our family vacation soon after he completed outpatient treatment.

"I began to learn all I could about the disease of alcoholism. I attended A.A. meetings with him. Over the next three and a half years, he would relapse more times than I could count. I eventually built a spreadsheet to keep track of his treatments. I became so involved in his illness that I neglected my own mental, physical, emotional and spiritual health."

All schemes to get your loved one sober seem well-founded at first. Those ideas are right on target in your opinion, but let's not forget it's *your* target. The addict's goal is to maintain a relationship with substances without getting caught. Period. Your ideas, schemes, and sober goals for your son are temporary fixes for your out-of-control emotions.

It's vital for you to turn towards those out-of-control feelings, give them a name, a label. I call them the *feelings of powerlessness* and experiencing them feels wretched. Allowing yourself to feel those heavy-hearted emotions instead of running away from them is what creates the bedrock of your healing. With a recovery program to mentor and guide you through what feels like peril, you will learn to trust in the process and in your own ability to make new and healthier choices.

Taking addiction out of its box, seeing it through a more compassionate, non-judgmental frame, viewing it as the illness it is, will lessen your guilt and allow you more freedom to do your work. Addiction is a treatable disorder and one that you are not responsible for curing. Viewing substance dependence as a physiological process happening inside the body of your loved one can help you call checkmate early in the game. It will dramatically decrease the time and the means by which your addict can manipulate and move you across the chessboard of codependency.

Your recovery lies dormant until you align yourself with that new framework. What you want is a different approach to deal with the pain. And guess what? You can begin your journey of healing without permission from your addicted loved one. You don't have to wait. Make that decision on your own, for yourself. Make it when you become saturated with all the old ways. Here's a recovery slogan to tuck in your psyche: *Nothing changes until something changes.* That something is *you*.

Magic Word is NO

A boundary is like a line drawn in the addict's sand. It separates his behavior from yours. Saying *NO* to unreasonable requests from your active addict can be the start of holding him or her accountable. Saying *NO* is the beginning of your right and responsibility to set yourself apart from your loved one's choices. And rest assured, your addicted loved one despises boundaries. So you'll need to be brave and let the addict hurt. Let him fail. Let her cry. Let her beg. Let her feel embarrassed and ashamed. Let her feel the pain of withdrawal. Let him make the phone call regarding treatment options. Let him be homeless. Let him get skinny as a pole while he's choosing dope over food. An addict does not reach out for healing without feeling the pain incurred by his addictive lifestyle.

Jane's story

"I realized my life had become unmanageable when I began having panic attacks several times a week. I was afraid to leave my house, and for someone in my early 20s, my physical health was poor. Doctors kept prescribing different things, but they didn't help. Eventually, I learned that my symptoms were stress related.

"My addicts were my boyfriend and my sister. Once I realized how bad their addictions had become, I expressed my sadness and concern to them both. That did not get results, so I became angry. I withheld information from my parents about my sister's use, ran to her rescue, gave her money. Then I began trying to control what my parents did or didn't do for her. I felt like it was my job to hold the family together and that I was the only person acting like an adult.

"My boyfriend would be fine one minute, and the next would be passed out somewhere. One minute a good time and the next he was an angry, evil person. I made excuses for him, drove him places, paid for almost everything, did all I could to make things easier for him because I thought that's what love was. And at times I was convinced there was something wrong with me for him to have to drink as he did.

"I tried ignoring his lies, went out of my way to look into his work and legal problems. At times I would drink with him. That way, at least he wasn't drinking all of it. I had already tried hiding his vodka, pouring it out, watering down his drinks. Nothing worked. He kept losing jobs. I would get angry, and he would promise to change. And he would change for a few weeks; then it was back to the bottle. I felt like I was going crazy. My self-esteem was so low; I felt I was worth less than the money he spent on his vodka."

Remember that change happens when there are reasons to change. Pain is what makes the person with a substance use disorder stop, look and listen. Pain invites your daughter to stop for some moments, look around at her life, and perhaps acknowledge the mounting piles of negativity. Then maybe those piles will be your daughter's addictive "bottom." Perhaps she will recognize she has fallen from the wall of life's safe places and become willing to chase after sobriety.

Living in the center of your own life rather than spinning in the web created by codependency is full of challenges. But so is staying stuck and uninformed. Personal recovery invites new people into your old world, sheds light on what is real, holds both you and the addict accountable for growth and change.

* * * *

Story Pages

If you have completed the writing exercises at the close of Chapter Two, you're becoming more aware of your crazy-making internal processes. You're beginning to see how closely aligned you are with trying to figure out or change your loved one's brain disorder. You understand that your loved one's brain has become convinced of its need for pleasure at all costs and you've faced at least some of the lies. You've written briefly about your unproductive attempts at controlling your loved one's addictive behaviors. You're more aware of your relationship dynamics, your pattern of being pulled out of your rational mind by addiction, and you've learned how quickly you resort to codependent behaviors. Now it's time to examine things in more depth.

Your third story page: Find your legal pad, journal, iPad, tablet or computer.

Write about your "ah-hah" moments in this chapter. Can you begin to see and feel your attachment to codependent living? Now create a Story Page focused on ways your life has been impacted by your loved one's use. Look at the following areas:

Spiritual:

How is your belief in God being challenged? Consider the ways and means of your spiritual life. Consider your belief system, God or Higher Power, your prayer life, your meditation practice, your church attendance, your time in nature, whatever framework you have for creating a connection with goodness and simplicity, your way of finding solace. How is all of that being challenged?

Financial:

Now consider all the ways you have helped the addicted loved one financially: bail bonds, fines, loans, mortgage payments, rent payments, tuition, school loan payments, car insurance, cell phone, car payments. How much money have you thrown at active addiction?

Emotional:

What has happened to your emotional world (depression, anxiety, free-floating fears, sadness, anger, rage, deep shame, break-downs?) Have you entered therapy? What three emotions do you most often feel when dealing with your addicted loved one?

Mental:

Have you experienced obsessive thinking, breakdowns while at work, lost work time, isolation from others? Have you tried counting the alcoholic's drinks? Or spent time searching the house/car for bottles of alcohol or vials of pills? Try and estimate the hours in each day your mind has felt affected by ruminating thoughts.

Employment:

Have you called in sick, lied about reasons for needing time off, been unable to concentrate, experienced emotional breakdowns at work, been put on notice regarding job performance?

Relational:

Have you lost friends, lied to family and friends, argued with a family member over how to help the addicted loved one, ignored needs of other friends or relatives due to the worry and chaos connected to active addiction?

When you've completed writing, spend time and attention looking at your answers. Play with this a bit: If you were going to incorporate the answers into the drafting of a screenplay, what would be the title?

As you make progress along the path of changing the way you show love for your addict, it's important to take a look at the despair you've felt and explore more deeply your sense of powerlessness. The next chapter helps you name and claim the pain and will connect you more deeply to your healing practice.

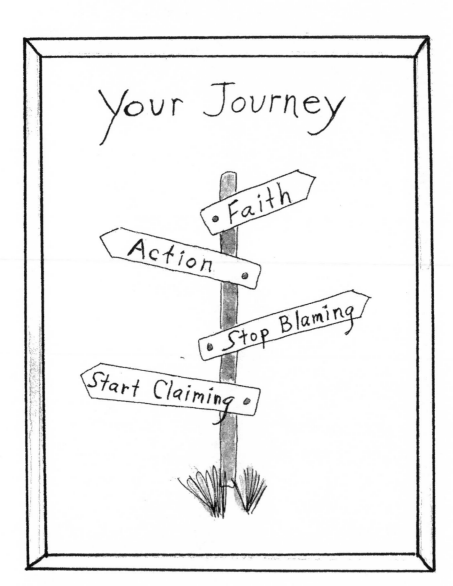

Naming the Pain

> Alcoholics just have their powerlessness
> visible for all to see. The rest of us disguise it…
> especially our addiction to our way of thinking…we keep
> doing the same thing over and over again, even
> if it is not working for us.
>
> ❖ Father Richard Rohr, *Breathing Underwater,*
> *Spirituality of the Twelve Steps*

Powerlessness. The three-syllable word that most of us would like to bury beneath the tallest mountain. Forever.

Father Richard Rohr, a Franciscan priest and founder of the Center for Action and Contemplation in Albuquerque, New Mexico, speaks the truth about family addiction. A sense of powerlessness grips both sides and exerts enormous pressure on both the addict and those who love him. The addicted loved one craves a drink or a drug and will violate his morals and values to obtain the feeling of chemical pleasure. Compulsivity remains unbridled, and the addict loses control of when, or if, he uses his favorite substances. Too much too often will eventually bring pain aplenty.

Julia Cameron writes in her creative memoir *Floor Sample* about a particular night her husband confronted her about drinking.

"You can't keep going the way you're going," Martin told me one night when he had arrived home earlier than usual to find me drunker than usual.

"What do you mean?" I didn't like being cornered.

"You know what I mean. I mean the drinking."

"You could come home."

"What's that got to do with it? You don't drink because of me. You drink because you drink."

Martin was right about that. I didn't need reasons to drink or even excuses. Self-pity was the rim of the glass: "Poor me. Poor me. Pour me a drink."

Julia writes about how threadbare her excuses became while her professional and personal values lay in a heap of painful rubble. Addiction is a coercive force and requires something to butt up against before the user pays attention to the mounting losses; that "something" is pain. Guaranteed: the chemical pleasure gained from the addictive use of substances will always be outweighed by distress and by relationship destruction.

So, of course, you want their pain to stop. Yours too. The loss of control you feel and the external messiness you witness as your addicted loved one continues drinking, using pills, or shooting heroin drains your patience, your bank account, your spirit.

Excuses run out, denial wears thin, lies become more transparent, and you can see just how ill the addict is becoming. And as the illness of addiction continues, you come face to face with just how anxious, angry, obsessed, and ineffective you are in the whirl of it all. Your notion of normal is turned upside down, and you find yourself as challenged as Sisyphus, a character from Greek mythology. He was sentenced to roll a huge boulder up a hill, only to have it roll back down and hit him, over and over again. The pain of powerlessness can feel like a life sentence unless you choose to step aside as the addict's consequences come hurtling toward you.

What is powerlessness?

The concept of powerlessness often gets a bad rap, particularly in a culture that is so bent on the development of individual strength and ability. Take a look at the word *power* in any thesaurus, and you will see it aligned with "potent, vigorous, strong, and authoritative." Now drift on down the page to the word *powerlessness.* The word drips with weakness: "impotent, unfit, incompetent, useless."

Our nation seems steeped in a culture of power. We are socialized to believe that our sense of self is connected to the cars we drive (paid for or not), or the number of square feet in our homes (paid for or not). We deem ourselves "good enough" if our retirement accounts rock toward one million. The media connects success to bigger-is-better. And after bigger, we'll go for more because we can never have enough. Conspicuous consumption drives our view of ourselves too hard and too long and too often. Movie stars or others who live with fame and wealth may play and live by different rules, but guess what? They become addicted too. Wealthy or famous people who become addicted all have the same road to travel: absolute realization that addiction is a killer, and sobriety requires a whole new set of guidelines to follow. Addiction is a great and humbling equalizer.

Our lives are scripted by social norms and, vulnerability is not necessarily a trait that merits respect. It is not a quality taught in our schools and along with humility, is best learned through our emotional suffering. Most of us learn to hold our hearts close, and we particularly don't like airing our family's dirty laundry. We stand prepared to go it alone, be prideful, keep it together, and get it right lest we open ourselves to criticism or judgment. Our culture has many difficulties embracing powerlessness as a place where strength can be found.

Addiction comes at families like a bull in a ring. Unless you are a trained matador, with a recovery program to wave in the face of the addict, you are likely to have your spirits gored or, at the very least, be hornswoggled by all the accompanying pain.

When addiction breaks loose in a family, all the prescribed ways of how we love, parent, supervise, and share our hearts and minds with others are blown sky-high. You can't stand in the ring alone watching the bull come at you. You need to reach up and out and let your pain and fear lead you to a place of balance. You need to rewrite your relationship rules, create new guidelines for if, how, or when you deal with the user. Recovery from family addiction requires the development of new emotional and spiritual skills, and surprisingly it is powerlessness that produces the path of growth and change.

Addiction, if allowed, will conquer mind, body, and spirit. Nothing is ever the same again. All you thought you knew about your loved one is up for grabs. All you have known about your personal strengths and weaknesses is also in question. You may have lived a well-tempered, well-controlled, orderly life before learning of your son's addiction. Your marriage may have felt steady and dependable before the onset of your wife's alcoholism. Your spiritual and religious life may have served you well during less dramatic periods. But after active addiction slides through your family's door, you must change your outlook. You must learn how to step back and allow your heroin-addicted daughter's life to cave in around her, and it's the hardest thing you will ever do.

Let's face it, being a mother to an active addict is different from being a mother to a non-drug addicted son. Being a wife to an alcoholic spouse will change roles and rules. Being a grandparent to a granddaughter who comes begging while she remains addicted to OxyContin or heroin changes the relationship landscape. Living with an alcohol-addicted parent dramatically changes the family patterns for young children and teenagers. While addiction reigns, so do the craziness, the pain, the confusion, the cover-ups, and the isolation.

Although you may already have been somewhat aware that you had little power to effect lasting change in another person, family addiction brings that truth to the fore. Powerlessness is, in fact, the biggest lesson for families: despite your love, care, and concern, you do not have the power to change your actively addicted loved one. All your anger, all your sadness, all those days spent pleading and begging and blaming brings nothing but more misery to your own heart. However, consider this truth: the pain embedded in your sense of powerlessness, that dreaded and vulnerable state of being unable to clean up someone else's life, is your most valuable asset.

It is also a humbling state of being. Depending on where your daughter is on the continuum of addiction, or how much pain, difficulty, and danger her use has created, this stage of family healing can feel crushing. Altering your focus is unfamiliar and disconcerting. However, if you are not to drown in the tsunami of dysfunction created by your daughter's addiction, a change of focus is essential; the focus must be on yourself.

An illustrative story:

Powerlessness was the topic for one of our Thursday evening family groups. The concept always resulted in many discussions among attendees. A woman in the back row holds up her hand, and I walk down the aisle with the microphone.

This distinguished older woman takes the microphone, and her hand is shaking. There are tears in her eyes and anger in her tone. "I resent having to be here. I've given my daughter everything. I've sacrificed for her so she could have money. And a car. I sent her to a private school. She dropped out. She was arrested last week. She's sitting in jail, and you tell me there is nothing I can do? That makes me even angrier. I'm even mad at the cops who handcuffed her."

A younger gentleman across the aisle motions me over. He takes the mic and addresses the mother. "I have felt angry and resentful many times. My son has been in rehab three times in the past two years. He's been in jail. I've bailed him out after he promised he would go to treatment. He hit the streets instead. I'm just beginning to get a grip on this addiction thing, but the cool thing is that we're here. Anger, resentment, and all the rest. What I'm learning to do is embrace these crazy feelings that fit in my powerless bag of tricks and not let any of them drag me back into enabling my son."

Those two types of stories were told over and over, week after week, as families shared the fallout of suffering. It is true that the state of powerlessness is full of naked feelings, the ones that make us want to hide, ones that make us feel helpless and vulnerable. The feelings embedded in our powerlessness to change another human being are downright unpleasant to hold. How could they ever connect us to a place of security or comfort? Seriously? Can sadness, anger, resentment, worry, confusion, fear, depression, shame and embarrassment, all those rocky, feel-bad emotions produce a healthier outlook?

Yes. And no.

If you allow the negative emotions to rule your life, they will wreck you. But if you recognize them as messengers sent by that humble state of powerlessness, they can form the foundation for the changes you need to make and for the boundaries you need to create.

You are not saying to heck with the addicted loved one, but you are saying *yes* to those dark emotions connected to your codependency. Self-healing means you will pay more attention to your own brokenness than you do to your loved one's addiction. You will stand against your daughter's use of heroin, your son's use of OxyContin, your husband's use of alcohol—and you will call a spade a spade. You will lean into the feelings that keep you painfully attached to the addict. You will take a bigger and broader look at relationships you have held sacred and recognize the dangers inherent in denying the dysfunction in your family.

You also will admit that you are riddled with fear.

The greatest fear

The biggest concern for family members who start backing away from rescuing behaviors and codependency issues is the fear of death. You fear that if you let go, detach, or turn your head death will come knocking. You fear that your daughter or son will die of an overdose—or be hurt or even murdered—while he or she is high. You fear that your wife will drive drunk one time too many, cross the yellow line and hit an elderly gentleman in the crosswalk. You fear late night phone calls. You dread your front doorbell will ring some sunny Saturday, and that you will see two uniformed police officers standing on the steps with news you cannot bear to hear. And you might be right. These disasters may occur, but they will take place whether you disengage from the situation or stay firmly connected. You do not have the power to stop tragedies from happening.

My niece died in 2004 from a drug overdose, and the family pain remains all these years later. Everyone tried to stop that outcome. She even made a few attempts to get clean. First was rehab in Ohio following demands of her employer and her family. She said yes to rehab, but creating a recovery lifestyle was another thing entirely. She relapsed soon after that treatment and went to an expensive inpatient rehab facility where she was caught using while on the unit. She eventually completed that treatment and then attended an outpatient program in her home state, where she reconnected with using friends and recovery lost its luster. She tried switching from narcotics to alcohol, cut back on narcotic use periodically, but was unable to loosen her grip on the death-producing mix of Fentanyl and the cocktail of opiates found in her system.

She died at age 30 from an accidental overdose, a young mother in her prime years, leaving the two young children whom she adored without a mother.

What could we have done differently to help her want recovery? There is much we don't know about the weeks leading up to her death, but this we do know: the yearning for life had to come from inside her. And we know she was a gifted professional, a warm-hearted, witty, beautiful woman who was loved and who was also able to procure enough drugs from enough sources, legal and illegal, to get the high she craved and the death she didn't.

An addict's pain

"*My name is David, and my first taste of alcohol was when I was a baby. My mother rubbed whiskey on my gums to calm me during teething. My taste for it grew into an obsession and alcohol eventually became a destructive force in my life for almost 40 years. I tried cocaine, pills, and smoked my share of marijuana, but my drug of choice was alcohol.*

"*My obsession came with a high price: loss of a marriage, friendships, jobs, money, dignity, and self-respect. I chased anyone away who confronted me or who wouldn't drink like me. I remember sitting in a bar one evening in Florida with a girlfriend who had been on my case about how much and how often I drank. That particular night she asked me to stop drinking and take her back to our apartment.*

"*Okay," I said. "I won't order another drink." I then proceeded to pick up the drink of a friend sitting with us and gulped it down. My girlfriend was furious and shot me that all-too-familiar look of disgust. She had already experienced many insane and obnoxious drunken behaviors and was at the end of her tolerance. She left the bar, and when I got back to our apartment, there was a note on the counter. "I can't stay here and watch you drink yourself to death." She was gone. Another relationship lost. But it would take me nine more years of drinking to reach a low bottom.*

"*I worked as a club manager, and it was nothing for me to drink half a fifth of rum and six to ten beers during my shift. My belly stayed full of booze while my life stayed full of problems. I drank to cover the fear and hopelessness, and my drinking created more pain. I lived on the edge of losing everything that is supposed to make life meaningful: my job as a photographer, my health, my car, my apartment, my freedom. Jail became a familiar experience. And I was full of shame.*

"*The end came when I was found unconscious on the concrete floor of a parking garage, lying in my own blood and vomit. I had no I.D. and no money on me. I was loaded into an ambulance and taken to a hospital. My blood alcohol level was over three times the legal limit. I detoxed in the E.R. and was encouraged by the staff there to go to a treatment center following discharge. They diagnosed me with alcoholism, explained it as a primary, chronic, progressive illness that would kill me if left untreated.*

"*I spent 30 days on an inpatient unit and began to feel better physically and mentally. I knew I did not want to return to drinking but felt fragile, so I went to a sober living house for six months and then lived and worked at a spiritual retreat center for one year. I attended A.A., worked the Twelve Steps, got a sponsor and slowly put together a sober lifestyle. I've been sober for thirty-plus years now, and my sobriety remains my number one priority."*

Loosening your grip on the addict can feel brutal. Standing back and watching the chips fall may feel hard-hearted. Of course, it hurts to watch an addict suffer the consequences of use. But it's important to understand that there's pain whatever choice you make: pain if you stay closely tied to the addict and pain if you detach. If you continue to hover over the addict, trying to control what is uncontrollable, the pain in your days will only increase. You can offer your assistance regarding recovery, offer to be there, front and center, for your son if and when he is willing to seek treatment. Tell him that. In the meantime, learn how to separate your pain from your son's illness and turn your pain into something you can heal. Seek knowledge about the concepts of surrender and acceptance. They are the gifts that follow your willingness to accept powerlessness, and they form the basis of your ability to detach, grow, and heal.

What is surrender?

At the outset, it's important to keep the concept as simple as possible. Think of *The Little Engine That Could*. The little train chugged a bit at a time, guided only by thinking he could. Your process happens as you chug up and down those steep hills created by family addiction. It is not done in a day, or in a month. It is a process of gradual change that occurs each time you face another disaster connected to a loved one's use. *The Original Angel Cards* Book, authored by Kathy Tyler and Joy Drake, defines surrender: "the ability to be with what is going on rather than remaining preoccupied with what might, should, or could happen. Let go of the need to manage life and deepen into the peace of acceptance."

Surrender is impacted profoundly by how you view your

circumstances. Try standing in front of a window. You will likely look through the glass, not at the glass. If you look at the glass, you will see the streaks, cobwebs, or dusty splatters left by last week's rain. If you look through the glass, the view beyond the untidiness is entirely different. You see a bed of zinnias, a redbud tree, a bird's nest. Maybe a lake. Or a young father in the park, teaching his four-year-old how to fly a kite. Surrender calls for you to deepen your view, to see beyond where you are right now.

Surrender happens as you learn how to stop, look, and listen to the pain in your heart and see beyond your old way of coping. Remember that pain is both a messenger and a teacher. If you stand motionless and ruminate or worry or come up with yet another rescuing behavior to save the addict from himself, you are looking at, not through, and are surrendering nothing. Watching the problem of a loved one's addiction through the heart and mind of your own recovery program gives you the tools and skills needed to do your work and will create change.

Surrender is also a deep-down realization you cannot do this by yourself. And the worrying you do should never be done alone. Each time you attend a recovery meeting, call another recovering friend, seek support outside your pain and confusion, you are surrendering a bit of yourself. Complaining though is a different entity. It keeps you stuck. Judging the user as immoral or sinful keeps your spiritual feet covered in mud. Taking your loved one's addiction personally: "Why are you doing this to me?" stalls your momentum. Worry, when shared with another person who knows the rules and ropes of family recovery, lessens your tension and begins to teach you a new way.

Both ends of the spectrum—holding on and letting go—result in distress, but detaching is more likely to produce a healthier you and greater accountability for the addict. When you detach, you won't be as apt to step in and break your daughter's fall or arrange your husband's therapy appointment. Feeling the ache in your heart doesn't have to result in you paying for your sister's cell phone. Learning to call a friend in recovery instead of attacking your husband's character when he comes home drunk, will create liberty for you and may also serve to land your addicted loved one somewhere near a bottom. A bottom is that all-important place where the pain created by the use of substances outweighs any pleasure the addict receives. It is a place of reckoning, and hopefully a place to start their own recovery process.

As long as you accept the addict's disregard for himself and others, he has no reason to stop using. It's time to become the mirror reflecting back to the addict the truth of what you see. When you stop pretending all is well when it's not, when you make up your mind to take better care of yourself, you are taking the shine of denial away and creating the groundwork for all to heal.

The saturation point

You recall the time your son arrived at the family picnic so high he didn't even make sense or the day your sister left rehabilitation against medical advice or the night your father was badly injured in an accident while driving drunk. Then, as you stand before an even larger mirror, that cosmic mirror, you also see yourself. If you hold still long enough to look deeply at your circumstances and emotions and all the ways you have tried maneuvering the addict with little or no success, the lesson is clear: You are failing. No more pushing the large boulder up the hill, only to have it roll down again.

I refer to that place, that moment in time, as the saturation point— the point at which you are maxing out on pain and are bone weary of having your inner world so woefully linked to someone's need for drugs or alcohol. It's hard to accept that your relationship with your loved one is not as important as her relationship with her drug(s), but that realization is necessary if you are to come to terms with what you can and cannot do to help her. You have felt the heaviness of trying to carry another, your inner world dominated by hope one minute and despair the next. You can't carry someone else into recovery, but you can allow all the negativity to move you to a better place where you can find healthier ways to relate to the loved one with a substance use disorder.

Learning to live with and counter the pain of powerlessness does not stop the hurt if your loved one continues to use, but it offers you a blueprint to follow as you walk the path of healing. The grace of it is that as you begin to accept the lessons of your saturation point—that crooked, awkward, wrenching, miserable place—you finally become teachable. Pain can be an excellent and grand teacher, but it cannot teach if you refuse to listen.

Therese Jacobs-Stewart writes about her powerlessness to create change in her alcoholic father in her book *Mindfulness and the 12 Steps*. In one of her many attempts to heal her family system and wrench her father into treatment for his alcoholism, a social worker contacted her and said there was nothing more Therese could do and encouraged her to stop trying. "I hung up, numb. Then I lay on the floor of the living room, unable to get up—cocooned in despair, alone, a bump on the side of the road while the rest of life passed by."

That's saturation. That's a codependent's bottom. That's an invitation to surrender.

What is acceptance?

Don't expect acceptance to be a twin to happiness. For families of addicts, it's a process that begins a step beyond your saturation point. Similar to surrender, it is a skill you will learn slowly, and one that will benefit all aspects of your life. The feel-bad emotions mentioned earlier are not only toxic, but they are also bossy. Strong feelings create a conscious mental reaction and condition you to do something with the extreme energy states connected to them. Take a look at three of the most common emotions experienced by families: anxiety, fear, and anger. Our negative emotions are like backpacks, and boy do they hold a lot of chatter.

When you unpack the chatter related to anxiety, the messages are predictable: "Something might happen, and it will be dreadful, and I won't be able to handle it, and I feel so alone, and nothing good will ever come of any of this, and I feel so confused, and I really don't know what to do next." Chatter begets chatter, and the more you ruminate, the more out of control you will feel.

Fear is next. "She may die, or he may spend years in jail if he is caught selling drugs, and oh, my God, I can't face the people at work today because they will know something is wrong by the look on my face, so now I'll miss yet another day and then I could get fired and then what?" More chatter produces more fear.

Anger is the big kahuna. It carries enormous strength and is particularly nasty because it's often directed at the user. "You are a loser. A waste of a human being. You've done nothing but let this family down, and I hate you right now. What in the world is **wrong** with you?"

What you have become accustomed to doing in the midst of all those runaway feelings is to get off your duff and do the next right thing to clean up the addict's life: give her money or bail him out. In family recovery, that is the last thing you need to do. The first thing you need to do is to claim and use the rules below before you act:

1. Never make a decision when you're in the middle of a toxic (bossy) feeling
2. Wait
3. Wait longer
4. Take a walk
5. Call someone who can hold the space for you while you vent
6. Examine your choices
7. Consider ways you've helped in the past and think about the results
8. Decide on two things you will NOT do to help
9. Give yourself a big star for not overreacting, for weighing in on change

Addiction is no joke, and family pain is far from funny, but some recovering family members have labeled those extreme and bossy emotional states as their visit to "Crazy Town." Humor can lighten your emotional load and allow you to form a new perspective. "Here I am again in Crazy Town" names it, helps you claim it, and allows you time to consider alternatives. Going to Crazy Town may have been the only route you've known, but it no longer has to be your destination of choice.

Acceptance of what you're facing becomes easier if you develop a means of counteracting all the crap in your head. Acceptance begins with your acknowledgment of those dreaded feelings. You can't unpack them until you learn to recognize them. Family recovery requires you to take charge of how you feel. You no longer need to allow emotions to dictate your behaviors. You get to choose what you do and how you are going to do it.

Let's do some more unpacking.

Bring to mind a recent time or incident connected to your loved one that left you feeling emotionally confused. Remember the circumstances. Can you recall the feelings and the messages? Was it anxiety? Was it fear? Was it anger? What did you do to care for yourself? Where did you go? What did those feelings tempt you to do? Did you consider your choices or run or take cover under your favorite quilt in the early afternoon?

Establishing ways to attach language to your feelings is a vital skill in family recovery. Keep it simple. Start small. Write down the list below, carry it with you. Pull it out during a crisis and choose the feeling(s) that best fit:

- I feel afraid
- I feel desperate and so alone
- I feel like I want to run and hide
- I feel uneasy and nervous
- I feel like my world is caving in
- I feel totally lost
- I feel confused
- I feel like a child, unable to sort through any of this
- I feel like I can't handle this
- I'm overwhelmed
- I feel like there is no God
- I feel like my whole world is going crazy
- I'm angry as hell

After you have identified the feeling(s), call someone. Tell on yourself. Ask for someone to listen and help you clarify your next step. Or ask a recovering friend to hold the space for you while you rant, rave, and blow off steam. That's how you learn to trust in yourself and how you gain control of what you can do to change your circumstances. That's how you begin unpacking your feelings and begin taking charge of your emotional world.

Accept the lessons embedded in powerlessness. Focus on self-healing and hold tight to the reins of change. As you create new methods of dealing with the whirl of emotions, you also will learn a new way to love. Yes, you can love and back off. You can love and become less available to the addict. You can love and state your truth quietly and clearly. You can love and mention that you are involved in a self-help group. You can love and tell your heroin-addicted son that as long as he is using, his life is his own and there will be no more rescuing from you.

And you can expect blowback. Your son may take note of your attempts at self-care, but he will not believe you at first. Why should he? You've always been easy to manipulate in the past. It's likely he will scoff at your remarks and will not stop using just because you've begun seeking help for yourself. He may change tactics, invent new ways to challenge your changes, but take heart. You have started to reframe your codependency by creating new rules, new strategies, and new boundaries.

Elizabeth's story

"The stress and chaos from his numerous relapses took a toll on all of us. I couldn't sleep. It was all I could think about. I lost weight. My blood pressure began to climb. I was ineffective in my job. I had a knot in my stomach all the time. I was continually fearful. I distinctly remember my husband's A.A. friends told me I was as addicted to him as he was to alcohol. I remember his last relapse well…I finally knew then that I could do nothing to help or change the course of his alcoholism. All that I had done (including neglecting my own emotional and mental health) had not

changed the course of his disease. That was my true moment of acceptance—knowing at last that I was utterly powerless over his alcoholism."

The razor blade

Therese Jacobs-Stewart quotes Tibetan teacher Sakyong Mipham Rinpoche as he likens the process of addiction to "licking honey from a razor blade. It seems like pleasure, but all of a sudden it cuts." Those cuts in an addict's life are what will create his bottom. Let your brother sit with his financial stressors. Gather your strength as your daughter drops out of grad school and loses her dream of becoming a veterinarian. Making sure he doesn't go broke, fall down, lose his house, wreck her marriage, mar her reputation, lose his job, will result in nothing but more enabling and little long-term change for either yourself or your loved one.

Your codependency will also create cuts. Embracing your powerlessness to heal another's addiction, accepting that you have been usurped by a substance, and acknowledging that you are trying to alter the course of someone's life at the expense of your health and well-being are invitations to change. A rebalancing of your world, that heart space where emotions connected to a loved one's active addiction have been ruling your behaviors, will begin as soon as you start making informed and deliberate choices. Those choices need not include making the addict's world prettier or smoother or cleaner than it is.

In the world of addiction and codependency, those painful cuts are where we put hope. It is through the cuts that the light can enter. Within each crisis, each loss, each embarrassment lie the seeds of transformation. It is important to view the pain of powerlessness as the recovery potential. Inside all those tangled emotions and behaviors is the uncut diamond of new emotional and spiritual skills.

It's critical to understand that change, which brings something new into being, demands that you align with others who can help guide you. People who are familiar with family addiction can offer a new perspective and hold your hand as you let go of the addict's. Remember that your love is not the glue needed to patch up your son's addictive lifestyle. Accountability is. Allowing the addict to experience his bottom, pulling the plug on all your rescuing behaviors, thus outsmarting addiction, is where the answers are found.

Actions

You are learning how to take a different stance with your loved one. You are learning how to take your hand off the hot burner of their lives. Rest assured that a different attitude does *not* mean you don't love or care or that you can't make helpful suggestions now and then. It does *not* say you want your loved one to overdose or suffer other crippling effects of addiction. It does *not* mean you won't call the squad if you believe your daughter has OD'd or that you won't keep a supply of Naloxone on hand if your son is heroin addicted. What it does mean is that you are learning about the dynamics of addiction. You are learning more deeply about your role. It means you are becoming willing to let pain teach you new ways of behaving instead of letting the pain of codependency overwhelm, numb, or freeze you on the spot.

It takes a while to see that, however. My sense of pain and powerlessness grew proportionally with my futile attempts to change, manipulate, threaten, and fix the alcoholics in my life; first my father, then my husband. My former husband was pathologically attached to alcohol, and I became pathologically attached to my anger and resentment. My emotions seemed to be *his* fault.

I put off the chore of accepting responsibility for my thoughts, my emotions, and my behaviors for as long as I could, and I became masterful at avoiding the duties of personal recovery. My tactics of avoidance included punishment—the subtle kind, using emotional coldness, pouting, and anger. I became a tried and true victim/martyr, taking each broken promise as a personal affront while holding tightly to my side of the codependent/addict teeter-totter. I whiled away codependent hours by trying to outwit the drinkers and by building layers of resentment over things I could not change. I believed my world could be tilted upright if they would just lay down their bottles.

Kyle's story

"*Her addiction smashed my ego to bits. Nothing I tried to do to make her stop using heroin worked. Money for college tuition was never used for that purpose. We helped her buy a car in hopes she would find a job, and instead, she found a couple of boyfriends that were not a positive influence. Looking back, I think my pain was as bad as, or worse, than hers because I sat in mine. She shot her dope, left the pain behind. I sat alone in mine until I got sick in head and heart. My business suffered, and my marriage failed (for many reasons, but this was a part of it,) all because I continued to chase my daughter around town, blame her, accuse her, focus solely on her getting better. I had become extremely angry. Now I've come to understand how to cope with the fact that it's her illness, not mine. I've developed my own spiritual program, and with the help of others I continue to grow, whether my daughter gets sober or continues to use.*"

You have become your biggest problem. It is time to stop blaming your addict, to continue taking a good, long, cold, hard look at yourself. Poet Mary Oliver writes about listening to the voice of healing in her poem *The Journey:* "*One day you finally knew what you had to do, and began, though the voices around you kept shouting their bad advice.*"

It's time for you to stop listening to your fear-based self-talk. No more counting your husband's drinks. No more following your son when he leaves the house. No more berating your daughter or threatening to get her dealer's number. (Besides, she has plenty of other sources.) As long as you keep trying to move about in the addict's unsettled world, your chance of finding peace is dubious.

* * * *

Story Pages

Chapter Three exercises have enlightened those life areas impacted by family addiction. Your choices are becoming more clear. You are developing more recovery language and are increasing words and ways to speak your emotions.

Your fourth Story Page
- What are your "a-ha!" moments from this chapter?
- What is your personal definition of powerlessness?
- On a scale from 1 to 10, how hooked are you to fixing your addicted loved one?

Now it's time for more lists.

List #1: Number from one to ten and write down the times you have felt shame or embarrassment in the past year over your loved one's use of substances. These include times you have lied to others about what's going on in your household or your relationship with the one addicted.

List #2: Go back to the list you made at the end Chapter Two, (ten times you tried stopping or controlling your loved one's use) and now identify what happened to their use *after* your attempts at controlling or stopping the behavior.

There has been much discussion in this chapter of ways addiction has played you. You have been asked to dig a little deeper into your own story. The next chapter will continue to guide your choice making and will help you set the stage for building that all-important support program.

What Can You Do?

Addicts and alcoholics will tell you
that their recovery began when
they woke up in pitiful and degraded
enough shape to take Step Zero
which is: "This shit has got to stop."

❖   Anne Lamott, *Small Victories, Spotting Improbable Moments of Grace*

Are you brave enough to allow the "pitiful and degraded" to happen? Author Anne Lamott has walked the path of addiction. She knows about those dark nights of active addiction and is wise counsel for both families and addicts. Taking Step Zero is what you want your addict to do, and stopping "this shit" will only come through a deluge of negative, painful consequences. Your granting your daughter's request to "spend a few nights on your sofa so I can stay away from the dope" will not be her agent of change. Your heart and mind grow more open to what is real when you admit you cannot recover for your loved ones. They must do it themselves.

Brian's story:

"Things finally came to a boiling point. My son called me to come and get him because he'd had a problem with the car. He was parked behind a strip mall, and when I arrived I found him overdosed in the front seat. The front end of the car was ruined, tires busted. I don't know how he had managed to drive the car there. I was able to rouse him, and his brother came and got him while I dealt with the car.

"We told him he could no longer live in our house but that he had options. He could live with a friend, live in his car, stay on the street, or go to treatment. We gave him eight days to decide. Three days before the deadline, he finally said to take him to treatment. I had already made the arrangements, hoping against hope that he would decide to go. I knew he wasn't exactly serious about it, but I thought if we could just get him there…

"He's been in a residential facility for going on two years. He's relapsed three times, but he's in a place where people really love and support him. He's trying."

My poem for my son:

THE WAY IT IS
I can hope for you, dream for you,
Pray for you.
I can brainstorm with you,
Encourage you,
Empathize with you.
I can walk by your side and help
Clear a path through the thickets and brambles.
I can teach you how to cast a fly far into the current,
How to rig a tent against the wind,
How to read the sky for snow.
But I cannot decide for you

Or choose for you
Or do for you.
I cannot find a different way to live for you.

Your addict's deepest lessons happen after he crosses over that invisible line of addiction. What was once a choice has now become a necessity, and the addict's thinking has become more delusional, his world more complex. Yes, addiction may claim your loved one's life. But he could also live through the days, become sound in mind and heart again. Only when he decides to stop using can the healing process begin. Recovery will deliver the skills needed to live in a deeper, more spirit-filled place, a place of strength, willingness, and hope.

Recovery happens as your son learns those skills, as he creates a life not dependent on substances. His drug(s) of choice will no longer be his guide, and yes, his journey will be full of emotional potholes. All the not-so-pleasant experiences hidden beneath his substance use are roosting somewhere in his brain, and they will come home to be healed. Active addiction does not increase psychological coping skills; it wears them down. Recovery will help him build a whole new skill set, more extensive and better than before addiction. He can learn to navigate his life differently. He may even learn how to love himself. But not during active addiction.

Whether your daughter seeks professional therapy or begins her recovery by attending A.A. or N.A. support meetings, rest assured she will find the appropriate leadership and mentorship in one or both realms. You do not need to be a guide dog any longer. The addict will discover who and what she needs to begin healing her addiction story.

You, too, have an emotional life story—all the marvelous and not-so-marvelous experiences that have imprinted your inner world. Your life story holds the texture and patterns of the life you lived before the blitzkrieg of your loved one's addiction.

No one has lived an issue-free life. All of us have our backstories, childhoods marked by difficult people or difficult times. Somehow we grow into adulthood but, no, we are not perfect mates, parents, brothers, daughters or grandparents. As you proceed with living and creating your recovery story, you are encouraged to meet yourself where you are, not to berate, judge, condemn, or blame yourself for any past emotional screw-ups, issues or problems, and to remember this new path is paved one step at a time. Your intention is the starting point, and your simple first step is to be willing to learn, to meet new people, and to continue choosing the path of healing.

The recovery road is full of perfectly imperfect people who choose to stand up to addiction. Recovering family members like you are a humble, confused, sad, angry bunch who are tired of having their human experience dominated by the addict. You are willing to open your hearts and minds to change. Staying mired in the muck of an addictive system hurts both ends of the system: your codependency will thrive and so will your family member's addiction. There are no winners, and everyone suffers. As you rewrite your life circumstances, know that setting the intention to grow out of your codependent role is nothing short of brave, bold and extraordinary.

You matter. You are important. You are a human being with a generous heart. You already carry intelligence and wisdom inside you. You can do this. As you begin to reshape your vision of love, care, and concern, it's important to unfurl a flag in honor of yourself.

Colleen's story

"In the earliest phase of our son's addiction journey, we enrolled him in an outpatient program for teens. He felt it was an overreaction. He blamed us for sending him there, said it gave him a stigma at school and that his bad feelings about himself were our fault for making him attend treatment. His use continued. Was it our fault? My husband and I are better than average at approaching behavior problems without impugning character while also encouraging ownership. Our son was not responsive to our approach. We tried reinforcing every thread of positive behavior and spoke with the best addiction/teen experts in our community. I took our son to a psychiatrist and multiple therapists. He just lied during sessions. He became an adult but continued to use. It took us years to learn how to detach and give him his rein."

Can you step away?

Is detaching from the situation the most loving gift you can give the addict in your family? Yes. As contradictory as that sounds, it aligns with the truths about addiction. Staying enmeshed delays the journey to wellness, as do all the times you have broken his fall and spared him the pain of accountability. Those snared by codependency try loving their family members into recovery by designing a life for them and by trying to control outcomes.

Ownership of issues is the basis of family recovery. *Addiction belongs to your loved one; codependency belongs to you.* Neither can save the other. This book states those facts over and over because they are worth repeating. Without incentive to change, why would the addict choose it?

Detaching with love is a core issue for family members, and your relational dynamics will not change unless you change them. You are a separate being seeking your way out of the messiness created by worry, embarrassment, fear, anger and grief. The message is plain, raw and straightforward: *You must step away.*

"What are you talking about?" you scream. "Get out of the way when she is threatening to jump off the bridge or throw herself in front of a train because life is just that terrible?"

Of course not. If your sister is standing on the edge of a bridge threatening to jump, you'll call for help. But if she threatens to jump while you are both sitting at your kitchen table after you've told her there's no more help coming from your wallet as long as she's drinking, it's her attempt at manipulation. And she's quite good at it.

So what do you say? "I love you, and if you feel that depressed and desperate, I will call the police or the squad and get you the help you need. I care deeply, but I will no longer ignore what I see going on with you."

Get out of his way? And let him die of a drug overdose? And leave a child without a father?

Although it is real that overdose can and does kill, it may or may not happen during your son's active addiction. Don't let your fear result in knee-jerk reactions or comments. Speak reality to him when you can and stay as clear-thinking as possible during those traumatic days. Of course, you don't want him to die of a drug overdose, so try asking him if *he* wants to die of a drug overdose. Put it back on him. Ask him if *he* wants to leave his three-year-old without a father. Tell him that's what you see happening and that you are determined to change your role in his addiction story.

Remember you are dealing with someone whose brain is compromised. Your daughter doesn't want to stop using because the high feels so much better than real life. She may acknowledge wanting the consequences to end, but she would rather find a way to do both: continue using *and* avoid the onslaught of negativity. But trying to do both results in failure. As long as use continues, as long as she follows the hedonistic call of her chemically wired brain, the avalanche of consequences will continue.

Confronting your daughter should not happen unless you catch her in a sober state. She can't hear you when she's high. She takes in nothing when she's drunk. Your husband is incapable of understanding the importance of your words during the shakes and sweats of a hangover. Share with your addict the day after the night before. Appeal to his sober state and tell him what you witnessed and how all of it made you feel. Ashamed? Afraid? Sad? Angry? Express your concern that his use has grown beyond any norm. Give examples of what you have witnessed. Caution: don't get caught up in his excuses, reason, blah, blah, blah. State what you witnessed and if the excuses begin, walk away, start a load of laundry, go to the library, take a drive. Get out of the way of his manipulation.

Daniel's story

"I had talked to my kids about the dangers of alcohol and other drug use and used all the risk reduction tools I had learned and taught others in my professional career. Utilizing teachable moments, family meetings, monitoring their friends and activities, but the one thing I couldn't do was watch them 24 hours a day. They knew

I was in recovery and that both sides of the family carried the genetic predisposition for addiction.

"As they grew older, their world and influences grew, and my attempts to lessen their risks of using decreased. I wanted to believe my efforts had not been in vain, so when my son began to drink and use other drugs in high school, I thought the subtle changes I saw were related to something other than substance use.

"Probably a perfect storm for what would become my enabling him. I justified helping him, and like so many other parents believed that I could 'fix' him. After all, I was the person that parents came to when they are experiencing a substance abuse issue with their kid, so surely I could fix my own.

"I spent a few years trying. Thousands of dollars later, after countless nights of worry and sleepless nights, after calling in favors from judges and treatment centers, and living in a home that had become very uncomfortable, I hit my bottom.

"I realized I was enabling my son. The concept of enabling I had taught so many others, but I could not see those traits in myself. I was preventing him from connecting with the consequences of his choices. I was finally able to focus on the wisdom to know the difference between those things I could change (me), and those things I could not (my son's addiction). Today I'm out of that quicksand, free from the false belief that if I let my son stand on my shoulders long enough, and tread the muck fast enough, that I would be able to get both him and myself out.

"Today I can say without hesitation, 'I love you son, but I hate the decisions you continue to make.' Today I am clear that my son is sick and I can separate the symptoms of his disorder from the person I raised and love."

Enabling or helping them stay ill?

In the recovery world, enabling means doing something for the addict that she should be doing for herself, but it's not that cut and dried, particularly in the beginning. If negative consequences—loss of friends, failing grades, job loss, loss of a marriage, health issues, legal charges, drained savings—have become a part of your loved one's use of drugs or alcohol, you will be asked to step up. Or you will offer help even before she pleads for it because you don't want to see her fall any lower. Your concerns and behaviors are normal in a set of very abnormal circumstances.

Your heart is trained to respond to another's hurts, and if you don't know that addiction has already set in, you may assume that your cash or your lectures or your anger will be the stitch in time needed to stop potential addiction from unraveling her life. And so you enable. You make it easier. Your heart is in the right place, but your let-me-get-you-out-of-this actions will slow her recovery to a crawl.

You can't begin honing the skills of detachment until you focus on how you have enabled, how you have made it possible for the addict to avoid consequences. Decreasing your enabling behaviors and detaching from someone careening towards self-destruction will not happen with a quick snip of emotional scissors, so it's important not to hold yourself to perfectionistic standards. Getting out of the addict's way, learning how to set new guidelines for relating to him will come in stages, and it's okay for you to choose the pace of your detachment process. It takes time and it takes effort.

If enabling is not so black and white, particularly in the beginning, and if the issues surrounding your addicted loved one are not that clear-cut, how can you measure where you are on the continuum of enabling? Start by thinking small. You enable when you:

- Look the other way
- Try hard to believe your daughter's lies
- Make painful consequences more tolerable for your son
- Make the painful consequences more acceptable for yourself by lying to others about your loved one's behavior
- Don't listen to your gut
- Justify, rationalize or minimize your loved one's behavior
- Delay getting help for yourself

Addiction stories are complicated. What if your daughter has little ones and will lose custody if the courts find out she is using again so she begs you not to contact court officials? How do you say no? How do you detach from all that? What if your husband becomes violent, abusive and threatening while he's drunk and claims he will kill you or hurt your children if you try to leave him? Detaching seems impossible. What if your loved one has committed a crime, and only you know about it? Do you call the police? You feel completely tied up in the situation. How do you escape? What do you do?

No one person or one concept can offer you easy answers to these kinds of dilemmas. There will be gray areas and questions without clear solutions. When dealing with complicated issues, it's essential for you to contact some reality-based person, organization or therapist to help steer you through these tough decisions.

What is your fear signature?

Your ability to change is enhanced when you become aware of your go-to response patterns to fear and confusion. How do you "sign on" when your son shows up looking disheveled and unkempt following a three-day binge? Your mind whirls. Didn't he promise to stay clean? Isn't he embarrassed? Is he going to die? What should I do?

Our three most common go-to response patterns to fear are fight, flight or freeze.

If your way of coping has included fighting, verbal jousts, shaming him or arguing, try changing how you respond. Anger and shame don't heal an addict. Your son has a ton of shame and self-blame already hidden beneath his use of substances. You can acknowledge your anger without berating him. You can turn away, grab your phone and call a support person. You can go into the woods and scream it out. You are entitled to your anger, but when it's directed at someone standing in the middle of a substance abuse disorder, it produces nothing useful for either of you.

If you are prone to freezing, numbing out during the hard blows brought on by a loved one's behavior, know that freezing your emotions hurts you. Those numbed feelings are not tucked away for good. They are apt to come out sideways, disguised as depression, rage, anxiety or compulsive eating. Consider the last several crises connected to your loved one's use. What happened? How did you handle your emotions?

Perhaps you have adopted flight as a way of escaping reality. You take cover. Just get the heck out of there, turn your back, go to bed, or change the subject when your wife tries discussing her concerns over your son's use of pills. *Running from the truth doesn't change the truth.* Running doesn't change reality, but it does remove you from having to call a spade a spade. With family addiction, it's either see it now or see it later. The facts don't change just because you won't look at them. Take a hard look at what's happening. Taking flight, ignoring the obvious, is another way of enabling the addict, and it keeps you trapped in delusion. It's also important to remember that you can't detach from something unless you admit you are caught by it.

You begin the process of detachment when you take the fear and confusion of your story to someone outside your tight family circle. If you see something, say something. Tell someone. The life you save will be your own, and in the long run, may produce the kick in the pants your addicted loved one needs. Remember that the addict is not thinking clearly so don't look to her for answers. Bear in mind that fear has a purpose, not to freeze you in your tracks, but to lead you down the path toward the people who can help you examine your options and offer support to your healing journey.

More from Colleen

"We wanted to trust our son. When he was a college freshman living on campus, we did not turn on our security system. Unknown to us, he would enter our home in the middle of the night and take my ATM card, take it to get cash, return it to my purse and leave again. All while we were sleeping. He knew my ATM password because I had given it to him months before when I had asked him to withdraw cash and pick up some groceries. He also stole a check from me, wrote it to himself and forged my signature.

"We paid for four treatments over a five-year period. Did we enable? Probably. But he could have been one of the four funerals we attended in that same time period. Four of his friends have died, and several have gone to prison or jail. All

from upper-middle-class, high-achieving families. We spent so much time not being willing to risk the life of our son, but he continued to take risks beyond what we could ever imagine."

Recovery changes your view

It's hard to see clearly when your story is being written by the addict. Who can see clearly when drama, intensity and fear roll through your life like molten lava? Stepping away from the heat and climbing onto a cooler, steadier landscape will offer you the opportunity to see where you are. Admitting you cannot trust your loved one is a huge step to take. Managing your fears while letting him feel the consequences of his actions is certainly not a talent you thought you'd need when you first fell in love with or gave birth to someone who is now an addict. Remember you are dealing with someone who operates from a place of injury. A brain on drugs is an injured brain, one operating full-tilt on chemicals, one that needs the pain of consequences.

Addiction to alcohol or other drugs becomes not only a way of life but also a way of thinking. Addicts who choose recovery need more than just a lifestyle change. Your loved one will need to develop ways of coping, feeling and thinking without addictive substances drenching his brain. And you cannot cope, feel and think for him. The addict has become learning disabled and must figure out how to deal with the ups and downs of life without the use of illicit drugs or alcohol. It's a monumental task, but possible for many.

Your addicted son needs to become teachable. His recovery will be supported by Twelve Step meetings, a sponsor, treatment facilities, therapists and from spending time with other sober people. It's important to remember that an addict in recovery does not look to family members for answers. He needs to value his life deeply enough to want to save it and to do the work of sobriety. It will be his decision, not yours. Let that be a relief.

Michael's story

"When my daughter phoned me and announced, 'Dad, I'm an addict. I need to come home,' I had no idea that I would begin a personal recovery journey. I knew nothing about addiction. Except for the pain I was in. I believe that when first faced with addiction, doing everything I could for my daughter was a kind of rite of passage. It had to be done. All of us do it until we learn that is not what the addict needs. Was it possible that I was contributing to the problem? It took two relapses for me to begin seeing myself as an enabler. I had to stop 'helping.' It wasn't working. And I was still feeling enraged, devastated and crying to the point of being advised one afternoon by a friend that I just needed 'to breathe."

"Keep the focus on me? I finally learned how when I began attending Twelve Step meetings and listening to others. Never before my daughter's addiction did I think of my well-being as even a valid consideration. How utterly ironic that dealing with the pain of her addiction led me to the realization that I was a worthy individual who had the right to be happy and serene.

"I learned the difference between support and enabling. When she called me after a good length of sobriety and asked for help to buy a car, I had to think about it. My first thought was, 'No, that would be enabling.' But she had completed a six-month women's program, was working and attending Twelve Step meetings, and was living in the basement of an A.A. member. She had found a job. I thought it through and realized my decision might help her sustain recovery so I said yes. It felt right for her and for me."

Small steps

It's tempting to compare your family recovery tale with another's but please don't. Each family story of addiction holds uniqueness, and each system will proceed toward recovery at its own pace. While it's important to share stories and obtain support, it is also necessary to recognize that people do not become immediately proficient at changing behaviors or navigating the emotions of family addiction. Love is at the heart of our human experience so redefining the actions attached to loving someone who is addicted will evolve. Start by asking yourself what you are willing to begin modifying.

Sometimes it takes a new action to change our feelings. Don't wait for the grief to leave or the anger to melt before you loosen your grip on your son's addiction to Percocet. You must forge ahead while feeling all the emotions wrought by addiction. You must become the leader of your life in spite of your mother's decision to maintain her active alcoholism. Little by little, you must seek new and different ways to deal with the issues connected to the illness of addiction. You have choices to make. Start small but start now.

You may be ready to change the locks on your house so your heroin-addicted son can no longer come and go and steal your belongings. But you are not ready to stop paying his cell phone bill because you feel it's important to keep track of your son's whereabouts.

You may say no to money handouts but feel empathy enough to give your daughter blankets when she chooses to live out of her car.

You may be ready to stop calling your husband's boss with excuses for his absences, but you are not willing to discuss the seriousness of his drinking with his aging parents.

You may be ready to discuss their father's drinking with your teenagers but are not willing to discuss the circumstances with your sister.

You may be willing to talk things over with a therapist or begin reading Al-Anon literature, but not be ready to attend an Al-Anon meeting.

You'll set your pace and progress will evolve. I entered therapy first and read volumes of material about alcoholism and family systems before I attended an Al-Anon meeting, and I didn't discuss my marriage dynamics or my childhood issues with a soul other than the therapist.

Looking back, I wish I had opened up sooner to more people. I believe it would have moved the healing process along more quickly, but I simply wasn't ready. What is important is that you find a place to begin changing, to take those first steps of separating your mind and heart from the disorder that brings so much suffering. Otherwise, your vision may never clear, and your own painful, arduous journey will continue unchecked and unhealed. Words of advice: be careful as you uncover your own story that you don't spend time feeling sorry for the addict. Feeling sorry for someone will not support truth-telling and will keep you tethered.

Rachael's story

"*I attended a support group for families at a local treatment facility where we talked about the chaos of living with an addict. I listened to each member share and made changes as I felt ready to make them. We tried everything, including paying for therapists and treatments for our son.*

"*I took it upon myself to get our son to Twelve Step meetings. He would stay clean for a while then begin using again, opiates and I'm not sure what else. We barred him from being in our house without another family member present because of all the items that had come up missing. Barring our son from his home was beyond hard for his father and me. He was homeless for a short time, living in his car with his addicted girlfriend in the dead of winter. We wouldn't allow them in our house, but I would occasionally give them a few dollars or take them food. Our son finally became miserable enough to seek treatment for the third time. I had asked him to let me know when he was ready. When he said he was willing I handed him my phone and told him he needed to make contact himself. I had made the connections for the prior two treatments.*

"*He is currently living in a long-term rehab facility and by all reports is doing well. My husband and I have received support from a therapist who specializes in helping families of addicts.*"

As you learn about what you can't do, you also need to look at what you can do. You can use your strong love to look the addict square in the face, claim your territory, and confront the truth as you see it. Feel free to use the cheat sheet below to begin reframing your responses, and then add your own:

- I love you too much to enable your use or to watch you die
- It hurts me to watch you ignore all the signs of illness
- I'm getting help so I can learn how to take care of myself

- I can't change you but I can change me
- I believe you'll want sobriety someday, but in the meantime I'm backing up
- I will grow and change whether or not you decide to get sober
- I am willing to support your recovery but not your active addiction

That last statement makes a stellar and irrefutable claim. You get to choose what you will do and what you will not do. It is your new way of expressing your love, care and concern. It also declares your intention, allowing your drug-addicted daughter to know you're not coldheartedly removing your love, but that you are indeed changing how you relate to her during her active addiction.

Any or all of those statements will probably bounce off your loved one at first and rest assured there will be payback. Your son may toss the confetti of guilt at you: "Yeah, well, you've never been a good mom anyway so why start now?" Or throw threats: "I've watched two of my friends die so is that what you want me to do?" Or pepper you with self-pitying remarks: "You're right. I'm a loser. I've always been a loser." Remember that these types of remarks come from an injured brain and are an attempt to jockey you back into your enabling position. That place is not where you want to be. Standing still as a stone in that one-down position only fosters more dysfunction. You're learning a different way to love.

Let's not forget the kids

Naloxone can bring a heroin-addicted mother back from the brink of death but what about the children nestled inside her addiction? How can those wide-eyed, innocent kids be pulled back from the brink of fear, confusion, hurt, neglect?

Dr. Nora Volkow, Director of National Institute on Drug Abuse, discusses children in her 2016 blog. She cites the importance of not turning a blind eye to the impact of family addiction on little ones.

Early intervention in a child's life where family instability is the norm can help stabilize a child's ability to self-regulate later on. Helping them cope and understand now also decreases their risk of abusing alcohol/ drugs later. A child growing up in an alcoholic or addicted household will become overly familiar with intense feeling states, particularly anger, fear and anxiety.

Opiate and heroin addiction creates family dysfunction on speed dial. While we're batting an eye or scratching our heads, a four-year-old is watching his mother die with a needle in her arm. A six-year-old is left in the back seat of a car or in the restroom of a discount store while parents tend to their drug habits. Children deserve advocacy. They need tender hands, a safe harbor. They need language, words to help them understand. They need to be a part of family healing.

Below is a short list of helpful reading material. Also browse bookstores or Amazon, and consider selecting an age-appropriate title(s).

+ *Wishes and Worries: Coping With a Parent Who Drinks Too Much Alcohol,* by Centre for Addiction and Mental Health, Lars Rudebjar
+ *An Elephant in the Living Room, The Children's Book,* by Jill Hastings and Marion H. Typpo
+ *Up and Down the Mountain: Helping Children Cope with Parental Alcoholism,* by Pamela Leib Higgins
+ *My Dad Loves Me; My Dad Has a Disease, A Child's View: Living With Addiction,* by Claudia Black.
+ *Understanding Addiction and Recovery Through a Child's Eyes: Hope, Help, and* Healing for Families, by Jerry Moe

You can also check your community listings for Alateen and Alatot meetings, and locate a therapist who specializes in working with children.

More from Carolyn's story

"Learning that addiction was an illness finally lifted the veil of denial for me. When my heroin-addicted daughter called me high as a kite to "explain" her reasons for leaving rehab after just three days, (she had begged to go there), I wasn't completely surprised. She went back nine days later, left when she was convinced she could make a recovery "on my own." No 12-step meetings and no counseling. Within a couple of years, she had lost jobs, totaled her car, dropped out of school twice, become homeless and was still using.

"The most devastating effect of her addiction was the neglect and trauma to which her daughter, my granddaughter, was subjected, starting with spending the first few weeks of her life detoxing in a neonatal intensive care unit.

"My husband and I had official custody of our granddaughter twice, the last time as an emergency placement. Prior to the emergency placement, my daughter and granddaughter had lived with us while my daughter completed the final stages of a child welfare plan. Within a few months of the plan ending, my daughter was using again.

"The cycle would continue. A bit of clean time. Promises made. Relapse. Lies. We did our best to hold her accountable. After months of legal battles, custody was returned to her despite mounting evidence that she was not sober. We don't know where our daughter is currently living but do not believe our granddaughter is in a safe environment. My husband and I both work strong recovery programs; else we wouldn't be able to cope with the fear and anger. I feel my little granddaughter's hug around my heart every day and know that it holds the brokenness that resides there. She didn't ask for any of this."

Your fifth Story Page: Grab your writing tools and answer these questions:
1. How do you relate to the information in this chapter?
2. What were your "aha!" moments?
3. "This shit has got to stop." Identify what that is for you.

Now the lists.

List #1: This list is an important one, identifying ways for you to begin changing boundaries and dynamics with your addicted loved one.

Identify ten ways you have held the net for your loved one, stopped his/her painful consequences from hurting too much or too long. How have you tried righting her wrongs (bailing her out, buying into lies and cover-ups, handing over rent/mortgage money, overlooking bloodshot eyes or constricted pupils or boozy breath)?

List #2: Identify ten ways your loved one has made attempts at creating positive changes, i.e., stopping use, Twelve Step meetings, dropping using friends, getting into therapy, obtaining information from treatment facilities, getting a job. Now compare it with your list #1. Who has worked harder, you or the addicted loved one, in trying to reach the golden egg called sobriety?

List #3: Take stock of just how much money has flowed from your checkbook towards the addicted one. Consider everything from loans to jail bailouts, to rent payments, to treatment facilities that have failed to produce sobriety, to paying for storage units, college tuition. Sit in front of these numbers and feel what you feel. Write down at least three feeling words at the bottom of list #3.

Next, we'll take a look at ways to widen and deepen the roots of your life-saving spiritual support system. Roots will hold you steady when the storms hit.

Building Spiritual Support

Destiny itself is like a wonderful wide
tapestry in which every thread is
guided by an unspeakably tender hand, placed
beside another thread, and held and carried
by a hundred others.

❖   Rainer Maria Rilke, *Letters to a Young Poet*

Rilke claims that our destiny includes becoming part of a wider weaving. Those 'hundred others," referred to by Rilke are needed to inform your recovery journey and to hold you steady on the days your steps feel wobbly and confusing. Enlarging your view of addiction and creating a new frame of reference for your thoughts, feelings and behaviors is not small potatoes. Redefining your role in your loved one's addiction and healing your codependent story gathers both meaning and purpose when you set conscious intention to develop your spiritual support base.

I like applying the word "base" to a growth journey. It calls up images of firm and sturdy, a place to stand when we feel out of balance. I think of home base. The base of a tree. A starting place. Solid footing. Your healing journey calls up the most vulnerable places in your psyche, and you will falter many times over. You have carried all the uncomfortable, tight-fitting, emotional family stories inside your heart and mind and subsequently your codependent behaviors have followed. Any consistency in your healing process requires you have a way to gain and regain the solid footing that a base provides.

Living with addiction has kept parts of you chained to reactionary behaviors and out of touch with your need for real conversations with real people about real pain. Your desire for a loved one to sober up, your time of living in reactionary mode, fuming, fixing and filling in the cracks created by someone's drinking/using, may have tapped your coping skills dry.

Constance's story

"*I am the mother of an addict. My journey has been long and full of pain. I spent many days, months and years in isolation, full of shame, fear and sadness. I never thought I could survive knowing the life my young daughter was living. What I didn't know while I was suffering alone was that I am not actually alone. Countless families are affected by the disease of addiction. And are talking about it. They are not seeking solutions for their loved ones but a solution for themselves to find happiness and joy whether the addict is sober or still using.*

"*A friend urged me to attend Al-Anon. I will always remember my first meeting. I cried the entire hour. I listened. I observed. I didn't want to be there. I didn't want to belong. I didn't understand the laughter or the fellowship. Didn't these people understand that I came to get help for my daughter? Clearly their situations were not as serious as mine! But in the midst of my pain I heard the words, "keep coming back."*

"*And I did. I obtained a sponsor and worked the Twelve Steps. By walking into Al-Anon, I have a life beyond my greatest expectations. Taking the leap of faith in trusting a sponsor and engaging in the Steps. Attending lots of meetings and embracing my own journey to recovery has made these the most rewarding years of my life.*

"I had to separate my healing journey from my daughter's. She's sober now! And the mother of a precious little boy. I continue to attend Al-Anon because the people in those rooms know what it's like to love an addict."

Pain is uncomfortable. It hurts. We want to run away from facing the sting of it. Our culture offers few models for acknowledging the upside of embracing discomfort, heartache or heartbreak. Today's society bulges with ways to avoid all dark nights of the soul. Stay full of food and you won't feel. Work long hours and your emotional world can be circumvented. Medication makes us sleep better and longer. Make lots of money and buy lots of things so the mind can stay caught up in the external managing of your life—too busy and too crowded to feel anything, least of all loneliness and fear. Our culture seems addicted to gorging, more is perceived as better, half-full is unacceptable, overflowing is best. It's easy to lose sight of what's good for us.

John Bruna in his book *The Wisdom of a Meaningful Life* tells the story of elephants and humans who become habituated to chains:

> *Just as a large and strong elephant can be tethered to a stake in the ground by a single rope or chain, we can be restrained by our beliefs about ourselves. Elephants raised in captivity and used for work are often chained up this way. The reason these elephants can be restrained by something as small as a stake in the ground is that they were chained up as babies. The baby elephants learned they were not strong enough to break free and that it was painful to keep trying to free themselves. As the elephants grow and become strong enough, they maintain the belief that they are not able to free themselves and no longer try...it is up to us to continue to tug on and test the chains.*

Recovery tests your courage, calls up those chains, asks you to strain against the old coping system so full of habituated behaviors. Let the pain of learning be an ok pain. It sure beats staying the same; at least these aches and pains will carry you to higher ground, to a process that includes learning how to identify your thoughts and feelings. Increased self-awareness is companioned by better decision-making skills and so your process actually becomes a win-win for all involved. Saying "NO" to an addict's request (unless his request is recovery focused) becomes your new way of helping.

I urge you not to foster belief in any ultimate point of healing for there is no actual place of arrival. That is part of the grace of recovery; we remain students. We declare an intention to stay involved in the process of growth and in learning ways to expand our hearts and minds. We learn as we go and we learn as we grow. And we are never finished.

You already know that active addiction is frightening in scope and intensity, but remember it is also invitational. The sufferings found there can throw you deep into spiritual and emotional dark holes where the only way out is through giving things up. Words make it sound simple: *give things up*. But the steps needed to walk away from codependent response patterns will not feel so simple. Give up the belief that you can heal another? Give up your need to control the outcome of another's life? Give up your need to be right? Give up your existential need to figure it all out? Give up your tears? Your fears? Your years of problem-solving?

Those are the chains. And yes, recovery includes breaking the habits of all that.

And giving things up can feel so incredibly foreign. All the "what ifs," and the "shoulds" and the "oh-my-God-this-family-will-fall-apart," all that familiar, fear-based chatter will file through your brain like messengers on parade.

That parade of fear and anxiety-laced messages are the neural pathways your thoughts have traveled for months or maybe years. It will take faith to keep you going as you strain against the chains created by all that chatter. Faith in the ultimate goodness of this life, despite all the untidy and unreasonable parts. Letting go of the feelings and behaviors of codependency is full of messy and irrational parts but interlacing the strands of those messy parts into a healthy recovery program will happen if you put in the effort. You don't need some grand, esoteric spiritual plan. You just need people, places and concepts that can hold court for you during your learning process.

Dwayne's story

"Ultimately we hit our rock bottom and found help with Nar-Anon. We came to believe that we were powerless over our daughter's drug addiction and realized how unmanageable our lives had become because of our focus on her. For three years before getting help, we struggled because of lack of awareness. We kept thinking we could control our daughter, get her on the happy road of recovery. We had to accept that our lives were totally consumed by her addiction; it was the first thing we thought of when we got up and the last thing we talked about before we went to bed at night.

"The Nar-Anon program promised a new life. All we needed was willingness. While we worked the program and developed new coping tools, our fears for our daughter actually happened: homelessness, prostitution, multiple arrests, time in prison. And she just recently had an overdose with fentanyl-laced heroin. EMT's brought her back to life.

"Working our recovery program helps us to not suffer as we once did. We have hope for our daughter, but we don't have expectations. She is finally in the ideal situation where she can learn from the consequences of her actions and her recovery is up to her, not us."

What people? Where are they?

Back to Rilke's claim that our threads are carried by "a hundred others," all those others are out there sharing their stories and waiting to help you heal yours. Your initial task includes linking with people who understand the family recovery process. **Start there.** Don't make it complicated. The recovery journey will eventually ask more from you, but keep in mind that you will progress at your pace. The key is just to begin sharing your concerns. Connecting with others is the first step up and out, of the secrets and the pain of your story. Here are some suggestions if you haven't already started to reach out. Pick one and go for it:

- Call your pastor. Let him/her in on what's going on in your family
- Contact your local Al-Anon group either by phone or online
- Tell the truth to a trusted friend who is not fully aware of the scope of your family's issues

Any of the above actions represent a change in venue for you, and that's how you begin the process of learning to love differently. Your life is your highest and best sacred gift. As you continue to build and broaden your support system, following those old calls of addiction, all those behaviors and feelings that have kept you unhealthily attached to your loved one, will begin to feel as unnatural as the old fear-based chatter felt natural.

Who are you without the pain?

It is easy to stay busy, so caught up in another's pain, or so mired in your fears and tears that you forget there are parts of you outside of all that sadness and craziness. What are those other parts? Where are they hiding? How do you take your eyes off the one addicted and begin reconstructing your inner and outer lives?

When it comes to you taking charge of you, of you taking ownership of your gifts and talents, answering a few questions can help. You can grab a journal or an iPad now or browse the following ten questions, then take a walk or do the dishes or clean out your car or dribble a basketball while considering your answers. The Story Pages at the end of each chapter, the questions you've been invited to answer, are meant to dig out parts of you buried by your lopsided love for your addicted family member. Story Pages are your spiritual homework assignments. Do not feel intimidated by the list of questions that follow. You are ready to provide answers. Go slow. Give them consideration and thought as you go about your days. When you feel ready, have at the list. Providing answers that only you can provide is a critical step into self-inquiry and self-knowledge:

- What are your gifts and talents?
- What/who inspires you?
- What places calmed you as a child and what places calm you now?
- What gets in the way of you telling the truth?
- What gets in the way of you holding the addict accountable?
- Who is your primary emotional support?
- What do you do with your fears?
- What is it that you most fear?
- Who is God to you and what can God *do* for you?
- How do you pray or do you?

When you've cleaned enough, or dribbled enough, or walked enough, or taken that last dish out of the dishwasher and tucked it neatly in the cupboard, write out your answers. Getting to know those parts of yourself drowned out or dumbed down by your strong attachment to a loved one's illness will enliven you and leave you wanting more. More you. More freedom to function outside the parameters created by codependency. More joy in living a life not controlled or manipulated by another. Your answers to the questions are a way to begin drawing on a new perspective, a new frame of mind. The energy and the intention to create more trust in yourself and more trust in the process of growth and healing is exponentially boosted as you learn to change your thinking. Consider this: your creation of a new way of being in relationship with your loved one is like a muscle that needs to be stretched and flexed. That's what a spiritual and supportive practice does; it flexes your thinking, strengthens your resolve, helps you construct new ways of looking at the old world.

Spiritual Base Includes Religion?

Developing a spiritual support base for your recovery may or may not include religion. Indeed, much strength can be found in traditional religious practice, but I'm also asking you to think outside the box. There is not just one tried-and-true way for personal growth to occur. There are many. If you seek solace and comfort through religious structures, keep your spiritual eyes and ears open for shame-based thinking. Addiction is not a moral issue. It's an illness that progresses. An addict is not a bad, sinful person, just a person who carries a disease that hurts and harms many. Make sure your pastor/minister or congregants are familiar with the disease/illness concept of addiction before you share all the difficult parts of your story.

My extraordinarily codependent mother offered her six children religion. We never discussed God in our household, never prayed as a family, but mother made sure her six children attended church. She would shoo us out the door on Sunday mornings, down our small-town street to attend services at the white clapboard Methodist church sitting just over the railroad tracks. She did not attend with us. Those few hours free of children were probably her time of respite. I think those Sunday mornings helped me form some notion of God, but not of surrender or acceptance of our chaotic and confusing alcoholic household. It would take much pressure, many years of not knowing how to show up in real-life love relationships, and a bushel of shame and blame before I could reach into myself *and* reach out to a God of my understanding. Perhaps my journey of healing was always bubbling beneath the surface of my days, but it gained momentum after I attended an Alcoholics Anonymous meeting with my father.

I was well into adulthood the evening I sat beside him in that church basement. I listened to the men and women admit who they were and what their use of substances had cost them as well as all who had stood close during the days of their active addiction.

"My name is Jack," my father said. "And I'm an alcoholic." I had never heard him refer to himself as an alcoholic, to give a name to his style of drinking. I teared up. I witnessed the respect others in the room appeared to have for this man who had hurt so many, and I somehow got it. I got that deep inside my father was a good person with a severe illness. I began, after that night, to understand that his healing included his daily need to keep track of his thoughts and feelings, his need to make amends and to accept that addiction could kill him if he began drinking again. I listened to him speak at that meeting about how he chose not to drink on a daily sometimes hourly basis. I witnessed peace so rarely seen on my father's face, and I was astonished. He had more peace in his heart than I did. We stood outside the church that evening, and I told him that "listening to real people share real, raw stories felt like being in a kind of church service. It felt holy."

"That's us," he said. "Alcoholics are holy, but we sure don't look like it when we're using. We hurt ourselves, and we hurt other people. Until the day we stop long enough to look around at all the destruction. And then hopefully we can find ways to stay away from the poison."

Then he left to join his recovering friends for coffee and dessert at his sponsor's home.

I don't remember much more about the conversation, but I do remember something stirring deep inside. And it did indeed feel like some holy invitation. Those men and women at the meeting reminded me of the story of *The Velveteen Rabbit* I had read so often to my children when they were small. Those people at the meeting admitted to living scruffy lives, to being rubbed worn by their time spent in active addiction. And they admitted failing in so many ways, as fathers, as husbands, as wives, as mothers, as employees, as friends. Attending the A.A. meeting with my father was a game changer, propelling me into therapy (where I grieved my story) and into Al-Anon (where I shared my story) and into lots of reading material (where I continued to learn about my own codependent story). Just going to church was not enough for me. Just attending Al-Anon was not sufficient for me. Just reading all I could get my hands on was not enough for me. I did them all.

You each have to find your way into the heart of your healing. As I've stressed throughout these pages, codependent thinking does not loosen reins quickly. Those behaviors and those feelings are not just hauled away from your psyche. The journey does not culminate by tossing all the old ways of responding into a trash container to be dumped in some spiritual compost pile. The journey takes practice. Those codependent traits can come flooding back, and creating your spiritual support base can help you build three important constructs:

- Build mental immunity
- Create a trusting relationship with your God
- Form positive relationships with others who can support your changes

Your spiritual base is your life saver, your life raft, your way of staying safe as your journey heads in a new direction.

His Holiness, the Dali Lama, discusses mental immunity with his beloved friend, Archbishop Desmond Tutu in *The Book of Joy*. He is not addressing addiction per se, but he does touch on the emotions that can shred our ability to experience peace of heart and mind:

> *Mental immunity is just learning to avoid the destructive emotions and to develop the positive ones. First, we must understand the mind-- there are so many different states of mind---the diverse thoughts and emotions we experience on a daily basis. Some of these thoughts and emotions are harmful, even toxic, while others are healthy and healing... mental immunity creates a healthy disposition of the mind so that it will be less susceptible to negative thoughts and feelings.*

Those negative thoughts and feelings require a firm resolve from you to put them to rest because they are what have driven your rescuing behaviors, which have kept you from the realization that you cannot play God in someone else's life. In recovery language, those thoughts and feelings have been the "junkie driving your bus." Most of what you have thought and most of what you have done in the past to hold the fort for your loved one is considered harmful as you move forward.

Acknowledging you cannot create deep and long-lasting recovery for your wife, mother, brother, husband, sister, son or daughter.

Doing the work

As you go forward and create new habits to replace the old, cold, undesirable, broken-down habits of codependency you must also create deep intentionality. Intentionality is where the change in consciousness begins. Saying you are going to change and doing the work of change are two different mindsets. One is a non-active mindset and the other is where all the riches are found.

Compare recovery intentions to dietary changes. You begin looking through cookbooks non-stop for new, healthy recipes to bump you out of the doldrums of cooking the same old meals. You can either read cookbooks, more cookbooks and more cookbooks, take delight in the beautiful pictures and ideas while you eat tuna from a can or fry yet another potato, or you can begin to create new meals. *Learning to Love Differently* asks you to create.

Create a practice that will support the new you. There are five components to building this new learn-as-you-go program.

1. **Pay Attention/Declare Intention.** Daily practice is important. Spiritual practice is built by reading books about wellness, growth, spirituality AND choosing to put the principles discussed in those books into your daily behaviors. Gather information about you as if your recovery life depended on it. Because it does. Declaring to yourself on a daily basis that you want a new and different inner and outer life is a grand place to start. "I want to change. I want to heal. I want to create more peace of mind. I want to develop new friends and new ways of being in my life." Stating intentions aloud, writing them down, sharing them with a trusted recovery friend puts fuel beneath your fire. Remember that all recovery needs is for you begin,

and it starts with the *intention* to develop new strategies for living and loving differently.

2. **Develop supportive structures.** Find your places. Find your people. Find your groups. Al-Anon can help you create a new outlook, can help you take your eyes off the addicted loved one, can become part of your new framework. There are thousands of meetings all around the world, and those meetings do a lot of things right. They can feel foreign at first, but I encourage you to read all their literature and attend different Al-Anon meetings to see if you can find a good fit. The Twelve Steps of Al-Anon can be deep and abiding ways to build your trust in God, yourself and others. You can also find education groups in your community. Treatment facilities often have education/support groups for family members and may allow persons to attend who do not have a loved one in treatment there. You do not have to share your story at first, just sit and listen to others share theirs. You will soon hear parts of your own.

3. **Acknowledge your strengths and your weaknesses.** You already know a lot about your story, about how you have tried to control outcomes. Make a list of the temptations you know you will face, e.g., when he accuses you of not loving him or when she cries and begs and asks for "just one more loan." Acknowledge your guilt buttons in particular. Remember that addicted loved ones are masters at *producing* and *orchestrating* your guilt because it benefits them. Make a list of what you feel most guilty about when it comes to your addicted loved one and share that list with someone you trust to hear it without judging it. Also, make a list of your strengths. Boast about those parts of yourself you are proudest of: the ways you have shown up courageously and creatively in the world, the things you have accomplished despite all the addiction around you. You will be surprised.

4. **Explore readings on faith/spirituality/wellness.** Al-Anon is not the only way to create a support structure, but it can be an important component. What I have found fascinating is that

the Al-Anon principles are inherent in so many mindful and spiritual practices! The language used may be slightly different, but the principles of detaching, letting go, forgiveness, and developing a relationship with a power greater than self is at the base of spiritual development across a variety of spiritual and religious landscapes. So the more you explore and read and talk and share, the more likely you are to hit upon the best fit for you. Your basic need involves developing trust in the process of letting go of your old behaviors, setting the intention to let go of controlling your loved one's addictive behaviors, and in your willingness to relish the sacredness of your own life.

5. **Redefine the word happy.** Some 30 plus years ago, I attended the First National Conference on Codependency held in Scottsdale, Arizona. I was fortunate to sit in a four-hour seminar led by Angeles Arrien, Ph.D., a teacher, author and cultural anthropologist whose lecture was focused on humanity's definition of happiness. She had spent seven years researching the concept of happiness cross-culturally, and four notions kept arising in her research study.

The first notion was LOVE. No matter the country, region, race, socioeconomic status, all humans in the study communicated their need to give and receive love. We need to know we are worth loving and are more content when we are lovingly connected to friends and family. How deep and solid are your connections?

The second was WORK. Angeles Arrien did not define work as vocation or career. She connected the word work to meaning and purpose in one's life, which may or may not be attached to one's way of making money. A black woman from Uganda might find her meaning in the simple-but-harsh duties of providing care for her family. An undereducated male working at a low-paying job in small-town America might define his meaning and purpose differently than Bill Gates. How do you define yours?

The third was PLAY. What do you do to relax? To let down? To forget all the stressors? When was the last time you skipped down a sidewalk? Or chuckled with a three-year-old? How do you stop taking life so darn seriously? What does your recreation calendar look like?

The fourth notion was SOLITUDE. How much quiet/alone time do you have in your days? Time to listen to the wind or watch the moon floating in the sky. Time to sit without responsibility. Time to unplug. Time to just be. None of us can claim victory or balance in all these areas but take a look at them and decide where you fall short. Take them one at a time, and decide where you can begin to serve yourself more from each area.

More from *Shelley's story*, the newlywed you met in
Chapter Two on building her support system:

"My husband tried counseling and was hospitalized a few times for alcohol poisoning. He finally went to an inpatient treatment facility and that is when my life began changing for the better. I found help in the Family Education group that met weekly. Although I had a strong faith background before marrying my husband, I had also grown up in a household where my father's alcoholism was never discussed outside home. I think we all believed that Dad couldn't get enough of the self-care information; I was living my life around my husband's addiction to alcohol and was caught up in the craziness that was swallowing me whole. I spent time in prayer. I prayed during my daily yoga practice. I spent a lot of time in nature. The group I attended was full of women and men who were also living with active addiction, and they helped me focus, helped me move on without trying to solve my husband's problems. I attended Al-Anon briefly but never found a good fit for me. My strength came from prayer and the Education/Aftercare group. Building relationships with those people who never judged, who never gave advice, who listened and shared from their hearts helped me build a new life no longer based on whether my husband chose to drink again."

A reminder that your support system does not have to be a twin to another's.

More from *Kyle,* the father you met in Chapter Four:

"I think I've always been looking for peace. My daughter's addiction became my ticket to growth. As I began to realize I could not square up my daughter's life, my anger was intense. I had to employ faith (many times blind faith). The Twelve Steps of Al-Anon became my approach as I became willing to expand my thinking. Getting over the anger I had upon entering the rooms of Al-Anon was difficult. It took most of my first year to do so. If I was to try and influence someone's recovery, I think I would suggest going to meetings, Al-Anon or other support groups for a year without evaluating what's going on in them. We come into recovery so beat up that listening and changing are very difficult. But once you start working the process, the process begins to work you. Al-Anon meetings have been a large part of my recovery process and so have other support groups. I developed a desire to read lots of spiritual literature and my recovery has taken some amazing twists and turns. I have now started a meditation practice and one of the most important aspects of my life today is that I know that I am the biggest problem in my world. One of my favorite paragraphs from the Big Book of Alcoholics Anonymous concludes "I need to concentrate not so much on what needs to be changed in the world but on what needs to be changed in me and in my attitudes."

Your recovery journey depends on you accepting the challenges of change. Yes, you will find your own pace. But you need to *work* at finding it. Don't hesitate. On a daily basis, do something to acknowledge your intention. Daily meditation readings from any number of books available on the topic of recovery and change can serve as a gentle guide. And yes I'm a journal fanatic, and I believe writing out your thoughts and feelings on a regular basis is a valuable tool. Finding a group of support people, a therapist, a sponsor in Al-Anon, a pastor who understands addiction will speed you along your path. Reading this book and then staying isolated with your own thoughts as you ruminate over your loved one's choices will take you nowhere. And fast. You've come too far to go nowhere fast.

I suggest you revisit your Story Page answers from time to time. Remind yourself of the journey you started and of the progress you're making. As a way of focusing briefly on how you've already begun to change, I suggest you pick up a pen, pencil, Ipad or computer and give a quick reply to these questions:

1. Who am I?
2. What have I learned?
3. What does my current support system look like?
4. Where and how does my support system need to grow?

I close with a stanza from a poem entitled *New Year Resolve* by May Sarton.

The time has come
To stop allowing the clutter
To clutter my mind
Like dirty snow,
Shove it off and find
Clear time, clear water.

Peace to you and high regard for you as you create clear time, clear water, as you clear away those ill-fitting codependent ties that have bound you. This is your life and yes, you can heal it. And yes, your own healing can take place while you also love the person with a substance use disorder.

Amen.

Epilogue

The Illness That Keeps on Giving

My father experienced 27 years of sobriety before relapsing. It started small, only a six-pack of beer purchased at Speedway. He was soon drinking massive amounts of his favorite whiskey and the illness of alcoholism began winning again. He drank heavily until health conditions called all drinking to a halt. He developed cancer and died in 2011 at the age of 88.

My last in-home visit with dad was a few weeks before his death. He lay like a tiny bird in a hospital bed tucked into the living room of his apartment. One of my brothers had moved in to serve as primary caregiver.

"I'm trying my damndest to die," he said. His voice was raspy and not much above a whisper. "Look in that little room. I've not done many things right, but I've got plants. Take as many as you want." He lifted his pencil-thin arm and pointed down the hall of his small apartment.

When I opened the door to "that little room," actually a spare bedroom, I saw that it had become his nursery. The room was his garden. It had several card tables full of opened bags of dirt. Dozens of empty Styrofoam cups lay strewn across the carpeted floor. Between 40 and 50 cups stood in rows, crowded onto makeshift shelves in front of the window. Each cup held one violet leaf sticking up out of the dirt. Dad's gardens had always been his way of doing right. Drunk or sober, his vegetable and flower gardens had always flourished, and each one had been worthy of being photo shoots for gardening magazines.

His last gift to me was a handshake of sorts. I stood beside his bed after thanking him for the violet leaves and assuring him he had done a lot of things right. His elbow rested on the bed as he reached up and put out his hand, palm up. I put my hand in his; he squeezed, hard for a man who was dying. "You be good now," he said. I squeezed back.

My dad was an alcoholic. He gave me life, and he gave me a difficult childhood. He also gave me the strength to grow and to give birth to a new way of being while we both walked our recovery roads. He fell out of step with his, and I'll always be sorry for that. But I watched him soften, observed his gratitude, particularly towards the end of his life. This book is a tribute, my way of expressing gratitude to him, for all the ways he suffered and all the ways he healed. He was a good man who was brought up in poverty, a man who dreamed of things being different. Maybe it could have been had the vicious illness of alcoholism left him alone.

I wrote the poem below in 2001, long before I began writing this book. My dad never read it, but I hope somehow he is aware of *Learning to Love Differently*, and that his soul sits somewhere writing its new story.

A Book for Captain Jack

Chapter 1 Your dream of becoming
a pilot remained tethered
to the ground of your
Appalachian childhood:
walls pasted with newsprint
a mother's loose breasts hanging
pale and loose
under a faded housedress
while she spread lard
on crackers
called it lunch
twisted a hen's neck
called it supper.

Chapter 2 Johnnie Walker became navigator
while you crouched on the
runway of irretrievable things
sat on a John Deere
plowing grief underground,
thin threads of tobacco juice
dribbling all things lost
down corners of your mouth
while mother scrambled eggs
called it supper
bare-hearted children
fled like refugees
called it childhood.

Chapter 3 You sit now slumped over
eight decades of grounded flights
sob into your shot glass
tell the men at Bianchi's bar
about your oldest son
who flew an F-4
over Vietnam
won a medal
called it courage
handed it to you
called it forgiveness.

Recovery Intentions

Learning to Love Differently cannot create change without follow-up from you. Your recovery process is what creates health and well-being. Each reader will find a pace for wellness to happen but be forewarned—wellness does require much attention. You cannot read this book, put it on your bedside table, turn out the light, roll over and expect much to change. I do hope the words here have ignited your family recovery fire, and that the 10-point recovery intention list below will be helpful as you grow forward.

I hereby intend:
1. To accept that addiction/alcoholism/substance use disorder is an illness I cannot control
2. To stop blaming the addict for being addicted
3. To recognize I have played the role of enabler
4. To direct my own life, not the addicts
5. To stop, look and listen to my feelings before acting on them
6. To create a reliable, dependable and strong support system
7. To realize that codependency is not a fault. It is a state of mind and a set of behaviors
8. To express love, concern and hope for my addicted loved one
9. To remain committed to ongoing personal growth
10. To treat my body mind and spirit with in all ways and always

Short Reminders and Other Things You Need to Know

1. *If someone is abstaining from opiates and alcohol but smoking marijuana daily, are they considered sober?*
    No. Not in the world of recovery. Marijuana is a mood-altering substance. THC is the psychoactive ingredient in marijuana and users can become psychologically addicted.

2. *Does Narcan just enable the addict to keep on using? Should I keep some on hand?*
    Narcan is the brand name of Naloxone. Administering it will reverse an overdose of opiates and keep your loved one alive so he can choose life and recovery. Administering Narcan is not an act of enabling. An opiate overdose happens for many reasons but usually not because the user intends it. Perhaps he has been drug-free for a period and so has developed a lower tolerance. If he tries using the same amount he used before getting clean, he could inadvertently overdose. Or perhaps your daughter has mixed drugs, which was my niece's story. Too much of a bad thing and she died. Narcan can be purchased without a prescription in about 20 states. Prices range for two doses are around $100 - $125 or sometimes less. Because of the epidemic of opiate use, some jurisdictions are recommending that private citizens carry it in case they come upon a situation that requires it. Anyone who buys Narcan will be given instructions on how to administer it.

3. *Is it true that Alcoholics Anonymous and Narcotics Anonymous frown on those who attend meetings claiming abstinence but who are taking physician-prescribed doses of Methadone or Suboxone or Vivitrol?*

    Yes, some members cry foul. Those medications can aid the addicted one for a time, allow for the brain chemistry to readjust so the work of recovery can begin. Medication Assisted Treatment (MAT) programs will provide a timeframe for tapering clients off medications, and one-on-one counseling is a part of MAT. The timeframe for MAT is determined by the client, therapist, and attending physician. Many MAT programs offer onsite group support sessions, thus allowing the one addicted group support without facing criticism or judgment.

4. *How can having an Al-Anon or Nar-Anon sponsor benefit me? Isn't going to meetings enough?*

    A sponsor can help you part the Red Sea of recovery waters. A sponsor can attend meetings with you, encourage and advise, as you begin working the Twelve Steps. A sponsor can become your greatest recovery advocate and is only a text or phone call away. If you step on an emotional landmine and are in crisis mode, a sponsor has no doubt stood where you are and can offer stabilizing words; their experience is invaluable.

5. *What about interventions? Do they work?*

    I served on an Intervention Team for a few years while working as a Family Advocacy Counselor at an inpatient/outpatient facility. Interventions can prove to be a significant advantage to the family. Often the intervention is the first time family members have shared their stories; the painful impact is no longer kept secret. Boundaries set in the family letters that are read at the intervention can begin a family's recovery process. The addicted one may or may not follow through with recovery and facing the intervention circle may feel like an ambush. Your daughter may bolt. The invitation is there for her to enter treatment that day and if she acquiesces, treatment can be effective. Or it may just be something she endures for some weeks and then resumes her use. Interventions should never be done by families alone. A professional needs to help family members do the groundwork and also guide the process on the day of the intervention.

6. *What if an addicted loved one admits he is alcoholic? Isn't that verbal acknowledgment necessary? And shouldn't that be a sign he is ready for treatment? And does an addict always need professional treatment? Can't they just stop on their own?*

   Admitting is not the same as accepting. It's easy for your loved one to offer words, but is he or she willing to make the changes necessary to support non-use? Accepting/surrendering occurs in the heart and is what will create a willingness to do the work of healing. Admitting a problem without a willingness to remedy a problem, isn't worth much. And no, a person addicted to drugs or alcohol does not always need inpatient or outpatient treatment. Some can just stop using. Much depends on the drug(s) of choice and level of life impairment. Some can attend Twelve Step meetings and do a lot of growing, while professional treatment or counseling can take the recovering person to a deeper level of healing. Sometimes professional services are sought after the addict has been without substances for a period of time.

7. *What about my anger, even after the addict seeks treatment?*

   Addiction is an illness. Hypertension is an illness. Cancer is an illness. Heart disease is an illness. The illness of addiction carries a stigma because it wounds and scars relationships and other life areas. The addict violates not only his own value system but yours as well. As you grieve the loss of what used to be, anger will be a part of that process. Find your circles of support, walk with those persons who understand your circumstances. Advice: feel the anger but don't feed it. There's a big difference. In my own recovery walk, I became attached to a saying I heard at an Al-Anon meeting: "Say what you mean. Mean what you say. Don't say it mean." That carried me through many an angry day.

8. *If my addicted loved one is suffering from an illness, how can I detach or cut ties with someone who is sick?*

An addict's behavior is unpredictable, hurtful and selfish. You cannot heal the addiction living inside the brain of your loved one, but you can heal the codependency living inside you. You may or may not decide to cut all ties. The key is to detach enough so you can realize you have choices. You do not have to stay faithful to all the confusion and pain. And don't forget, the addict has an illness, yes. But it's a treatable one. Treatment and healing are what you want for your loved one. Detaching with love, being honest with the one addicted, and creating new boundaries are just what your son or daughter needs, and what is needed to heal your family circle.

9. *What if the one addicted decides to stop? Cold turkey? Is that safe?*

So much depends on the drug(s) used, duration of use, and health of the individual. An alcoholic who has been drinking daily just to maintain a certain level of alcohol in his system should not stop drinking cold turkey. He requires medical attention to ensure a safe withdrawal. Stopping use of heroin or opiates, can produce highly uncomfortable withdrawal symptoms, but withdrawal from those drugs is not as dangerous as withdrawal from alcohol. Detoxing from benzodiazepines can be physically dangerous and should never be done without medical attention. I lean towards medical monitoring for all withdrawal processes, just be on the safe side.

10. *How long does all this healing take? How many months before I get it? Does it get easier?*

I've been working the principles of family recovery for 30-plus years and have concluded my learning will be a lifelong process.

The pain of loving someone whose life has spun headlong into addiction is full of great challenge as well as great possibility. It can become a lighter walk for you, a place bound by acceptance, faith, and trust. Those universal concepts will slowly pave your way. Yes, it becomes easier. Healing will form a new platform, a new perspective, and comfort beyond measure.

11. *What is the difference between clean and sober? Or are they the same?*
They are not the same, and there are many variables. So much depends on the user's emotional and psychological maturity prior to addiction. Other factors that will impact an addicts clean vs. sober state of being will include the length of time using, type of drugs used, and damage incurred by use. Clean means the user is free from all use of mood-altering/addictive substances. A user can stop use and not do a lick of psychological healing. Sober refers to a non-using state accompanied by the work of spiritual and psychological healing. The term "dry drunk" is used in Twelve Step circles to refer to a man or woman who stops the use of substances without doing the work of healing, without deepening in self-understanding, without broadening in self- awareness, and without increasing his or her range of coping skills. That person may harbor much negativity in mind and heart and be just plain unpleasant to be around.

Resources

Adams, Kathleen, M.A., *Journal to the Self, Twenty-Two Paths to Personal Growth*, 1990, Warner Books.

Al-Anon Family Groups, *Paths to Recovery, Al-Anon's Steps, Traditions and Concepts*, 1997.

Al-Anon Family Groups, *Courage to Change, One Day at a Time in Al-Anon II*, 1992.

Beattie, Melody, *Language of Letting Go*, 1990, Hazelden Foundation.

Beattie, Melody, *The New Codependency*, 2009, Simon and Shuster.

Brown, Brene, Ph.D., L.M.S.W., *The Gifts of Imperfection, Let Go of Who You Think You're Supposed to Be and Embrace Who You Are*, 2010 Hazelden Publishing.

Bruna, John, *The Wisdom of a Meaningful Life, The Essence Of Mindfulness*, 2016, Central Recovery Press.

Casey, Karen, *Let Go Now, Embracing Detachment*, 2010, Conari Press.

Casey, Karen, *The Good Stuff From Growing Up In A Dysfunctional Family*, 2013, Red Wheel/Weiser, LLC.

Casey, Karen, *Each Day a New Beginning, Daily Meditations for Women*, 1982, Hazelden Meditation Series.

Chodron, Pema, *Taking the Leap, Freeing Ourselves from Old Habits and Fears*, 2009, Shambhala Publications, Inc.

Hughes, Ed, MPS, LICDC and Turner, Ronald, M. D. CDCA, *Baffled by Addiction? Successful Strategies to Help Your Addicted Loved One*, 2009 GroundSwell, LLC.

Jacobs-Stewart, Therese, *Mindfulness and the 12 Steps, Living Recovery in the Present Moment*, 2010, Hazelden.

Lama, Dali, His Holiness and Tutu, Desmond, Archbishop, *The Book of Joy, Lasting Happiness in a Changing World*, 2016, Avery, an imprint of Penguin Random House.

Lamott, Anne, *Small Victories, Spotting Improbable Moments of Grace*, 2014, Riverhead Books.

Lancer, Darlene, MFT, *Codependency for Dummies*, 2012, John Wiley & Sons, Inc.

Nar-Anon Family Groups, *Sharing Experience, Strength and Hope* SEHS, 2009.

Rohr, Fr. Richard, *What the Mystics Know, Seven Pathways to Your Deeper Self*, 2015, The Crossroad Publishing Company.

Rohr, Fr. Richard, *Breathing Underwater, Spirituality of the Twelve Steps*, 2011, St. Anthony Messenger Press.

Talbot Hall Addiction Medicine at The Ohio State University, *Understanding Addiction*, (2 DVD set featuring Dr. Brad Lander), 2010, The Ohio State University Medical Center.

Quinones, Sam, *Dreamland, The True Tale of America's Opiate Epidemic*, 2015, Bloomsbury Press.

Williams, Paul and Tracey Jackson, *Gratitude & Trust, Six Affirmations That Will Change Your Life*, 2014, Penguin House.

Made in the USA
Middletown, DE
18 August 2018